HUGO

JENNIFER JULIE MILLER

ACKNOWLEDGMENTS

I want to dedicate this book to my husband, **Rick.** There are no words to describe my love for you, but the one thing I really want to say is, thank you, for WANTING me, and for being my HERO!

Also, I want to say thanks to my parents, my amazing kids, my beautiful grandkids, my crazy aunt, and all my friends for all your constant support. I want to thank my family for all the hours you have had to listen to the insane ideas inside my head. Even though most of you think I need to be evaluated.

COVER ART BY © CREATIVE
COVER DESIGNS (VICKI ADRIAN)
ARTIST

Beta Readers:

Lorene Palmer, Rick Miller, Ethel Nance.

Editors: Partners in Crime Book Services, Randy Henry

Photographs:

Brittany Henry & Rick Miller

CHAPTER 1

M iya

I was lying on the bed reading when Mom suddenly throws open my bedroom door screaming, "Get up, hurry!"

"Why, what's going on?"

"I have no time to tell you right now. We have to leave here in no less than ten minutes. Take this bag and put whatever you can't live without in it."

"Mom, you are talking in riddles."

She grabs my arm. "Listen, Miya, you are never coming back here again. Now get your ass up and pack this bag quickly. I have a few things I need to gather for you." I just stand here. "Please, baby, just humor me."

"Mom, I can't put my whole life in this backpack. Where in the Hell are we going?"

"I'll tell you more in the car, and make it work because that's all the room you'll have." She stops before walking out the door,... Turning back towards me for a second. "I would probably roll up a couple of extra pairs of panties, throw in some tampons, and don't forget your toothbrush. Layer the clothes you have on so you will have a few changes on you. This will also give you more room in that bag. Make sure to grab your favorite pictures off the vanity mirror, and whatever else you can't live without, but do it now."

She rushes back out of the room and I know I'm just standing here with my mouth open. "What in the living hell is going on?" I yell out.

I look around my room and my mind goes blank for a second. "Ok," I start talking to myself. "I will need…Chapstick for sure, as Mom said, panties are a must, hair scrunchies, maybe some Tylenol, and I'm not leaving the house without my eyeliner." I grab my favorite stuffed animal and tie it to the front of the bag. Then I tuck my Kindle in the side pocket.

Opening up my jewelry box, I start to pull out Grandma's watch, only to stop and put the entire box in the bottom of the backpack. Grandma had this made for me when I was little, and even as an adult, it's still one of my favorite things. The silver box has my name engraved across the top and a tiny ballerina spins around inside when you open the lid. I can't imagine leaving it behind. I yank all the pictures off the mirror on the vanity, grab my multi-charger out of the wall, and my cell phone. It's amazing how all the things you can't live without really reduce in number when you only have a single bag to put them in.

I run into the closet, pulling a few of my favorite hoodies on top of the others. Then I shimmy on a pair of jeans over my leggings. I feel like that kid in the movie *Christmas Story* as I layer my clothes… before long, I won't be able to put my arms down.

As I tie my tennis shoes, I look around the closet again. I grab a pair of gloves and then my favorite sandals, stuffing them in the small backpack. I have it packed so tight, I almost can't get the zipper to close.

Mom yells at me as she starts down the steps. "Miya, we have to leave now. I'll meet you in the car."

The whole house starts shaking as I look back at my room one more time. I grab onto the wall, terrified. I hear Mom laying on the horn and I rush down the stairs, clinging to the handrail. Pictures are falling off the walls and I can hear dishes rattling in the cabinets as I close the door behind me. Mom is waving at me frantically to hurry. She opens the passenger's side door and I jump in.

"Mom, what is going on?"

"I think this is just a calm before the storm, honey. Now, hold on, we have to get to your dad." She backs out of the driveway, barely looking for traffic before she starts speeding down the road. "Miya, I need you to listen to me. We didn't say anything to you about this before because your dad wasn't sure if he could steal the codes he needed to activate the pod. And we didn't want you to spend your last days here worrying about the unknown in front of you. He just called, and said we had less than thirty minutes before the codes are changed again. I'm so sorry…I should have been preparing you for this, but I think I was in denial too. All along I was praying for a miracle. I got what I was asking for, just not the way I wanted it."

"What are you talking about? Watch out, you almost hit that car! Mom, slow down before you kill us both!"

"Miya, honey, there is no time! You need to stop asking me questions and listen. The earthquakes, the intense storms, all of these things are just the beginning of the end. The politicians have been trying to delay people from losing their shit by keeping it all a secret, but the Earth is destroying itself. That impact that happened on Jupiter a little while back has screwed the whole galaxy up, and if your dad hadn't been working at the Space Research Center, we wouldn't have known anything about all of this either.

"This is our one and only chance of saving you. Now, I have put all of my jewelry and our silver and gold coins in the side pocket of that backpack. I'm hoping this will give you something to barter with. I know money won't do you any good on another planet, but maybe because the jewels are of another world, they will be worth something."

"Mom, barter with who?"

"God,… how do I explain everything you need to know in just a few minutes? Miya, aliens exist. There are planets in other solar systems with unknown species on them. They have known this for years, but once again, it was on a need-to-know basis. Your dad's company is considered the most advanced when it comes to space exploration. They were building and designing ships that they hoped would be able to travel those distances so that we could contact the Others. Damn, how I wish all of this was nothing more than a bad dream. And I hate it even worse that I don't know how to prepare you for what's to come."

"Mom, look, I understand everyone is freaking out, but I'm not going anywhere. I'll stay with you and Dad and we will go somewhere. I don't know… where, but there has to be a safe place on Earth where we can all go. If they can build rockets, I'm sure there are bunkers or something we could all head to together."

Mom slides into a parking spot and grabs my backpack as she jumps out. I throw the door open and run after her. "Mom, stop! Talk to me."

"Miya, your whole life is in front of you. One of these days, you will understand what you would do as a parent to save your child."

"Mom, I have a life here. I have friends. I mean, I'm supposed to go on a date tomorrow… A date I was really looking forward to, and—"

She turns suddenly. "No one on Earth is going to make it, Miya!" she screams at me. "You are refusing to hear the words coming out of my mouth. Baby, there is only a few hours left before what they are saying is a world-destroying storm hits this area. Your dad and his colleagues have been working around the clock producing these pods to save as many of you as they can. He only agreed to stay at work and help because they promised he could have one of the pods for you. This morning they pulled him aside and told him that they were sorry, but one of the senators was taking your pod for his son. That's why we have to hurry, piss on that senator's kid. Mine comes first.

"Baby, you have to live… for me and your dad. I refuse to accept anything else. This can't be the end of humanity or you. I have no idea if we are simply sending you off to die in space alone instead of here, but at least I will know in my heart that we did everything we could to save you."

Tears flow down Mom's face as she sobs out those last words. Dad yells at us as he comes running down the hallway. He grabs both of us in a huge hug before saying. "Come, there is no time."

Mom and I run after him as he takes us into a part of the facility I have never been to before. We exit a man door and head outside. Dark clouds moving slowly towards us have the wind blowing my hair all over the place.

Huge rockets are lined up as far as I can see. Dad stops in front of the third one, opening a hatch at the bottom. I no longer take a few steps inside looking around when Dad opens up what looks like a clear casket.

"Miya, put your back against the wall and tuck that backpack between your legs. Then I need you to stick this communicator in your ear."

I wiggle what looks like a small hearing aid into my ear, tears flowing down my cheeks as what is happening to me starts to kick in. "Daddy, what's going to happen to me…or you and Mom?"

"You are going to survive, baby,… and then we will leave the rest in God's hands. Now listen, you have not been trained to handle the G-forces this rocket will produce. It will more than likely knock you out, so try not to panic or fight it. I have no idea if you will reawaken in this capsule, or on another planet, but you are smart. Don't panic, and if you find yourself in a life or death situation, try to fall back on all I have taught you. I have packed provisions for you in this capsule, there is a survival pack next to your right hand… all you have to do to get it,… is open that panel behind your right hand. There is an oxygen mask stored above your head and an extra tank at your feet. Those should be good for a few months a piece if you land somewhere that doesn't have oxygen. I'm going to strap you down tightly, but once the rocket detaches, the straps will loosen on their own. The capsule will keep you asleep, almost like you're in a coma. I can't tell you what kind of condition your body will be in when you come to, as I don't have time to prep you correctly… but this is your only chance."

He starts hooking and pulling at the restraints. Almost every inch of my body is being tied down tightly. "Daddy, I don't want to leave! Please, let me stay here with you and Mom. I'm sure there are plenty of people out there who would love to escape all of this."

"Absolutely not. Your mother and I have been working on this for months. I refuse to let you die here. At least out there, you have a chance of surviving and possibly a life, here all I can guarantee is your death. Now listen,… wherever you land, more than likely you will be just as alien to them as they are to you,…so try not to freak out.

"Use that sweet personality of yours and your good looks for all they're worth. Find someone or something to keep you safe until you figure out your surroundings. But most of all, don't forget how much we love you. I pray one day you forgive us for this."

He pulls me close, kissing me on the forehead before Mom comes over, hugging me as tight as she can around the straps. She is crying so hard she is shaking all over. She kisses my cheek and I feel Dad pull her away from me.

Before I can say another word, Dad hits a button and I watch them step back as a clear lid seals me in place. Where I have been crying, there is snot running down my nose. I'm having a hard time breathing and I need to pee.

I scream, begging Dad to let me out. He grabs Mom around the waist and pulls her away. The last thing I see is her reaching for me before the doors shut. I hate being closed in and the walls feel like they are folding in on me. I start to panic.

The moment that door seals and the only thing I can see is the metal surrounding this tube. That's when it really hits me,… what's happening. Dad is shooting me into space,…alone.

The casket-like thing starts to shake violently. *Oh, My God, I have to get out of here.* I start to fight the restraints, only to be pinned back against the wall so hard I can feel my teeth rattling. I scream at the top of my lungs. My skin feels like it's being stretched forcefully across my body. A bright flash has me squeezing my eyes closed tightly, and then I feel heat flowing across my skin. Something bangs against the container I'm in hard, and the last thought that runs through my mind as the dark spots spread across my vision is that I would have rather died with Mom and Dad than out here all alone.

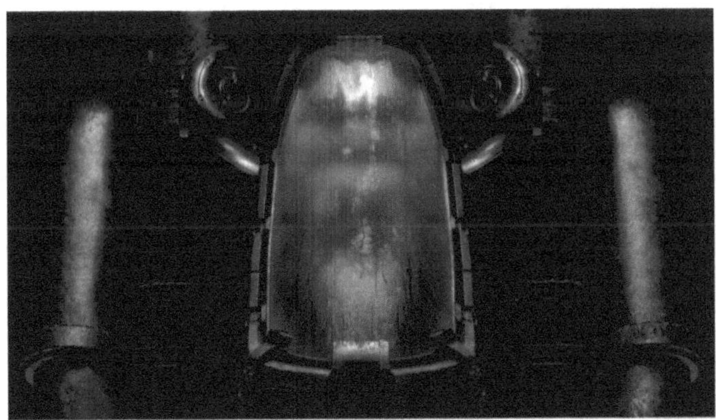

CHAPTER 2

H^{ugo}

I'm torn as I turn away from Tordan and Luna. Especially since I'm running back toward what has been my prison for many risings now. Luna has been the only friend I had in so long, it's hard to hand her off to another, but I know that male is her best chance of survival. Of course, it's hard for me to swallow my pride as I have to give her to what used to be one of my biggest enemies, the frackin' Darverions.

The sound of footsteps behind me has me stopping suddenly. I twist around, ready to fight for my freedom if need be, when the male that had grabbed me earlier cuffing my hands behind my back, yells out.

"Peace, man, I know we didn't get off to the best start here, but Tordan asked a few of us to come to help you put the fire out. He wants to see if we can save an AMI. Not sure who that is."

I relax, then motion for them to come with me. "Follow me. I'll try to explain on the way. I'll take all the help I can get, as I'm not sure what we are walking into. AMI is the <u>A</u>rtificial <u>M</u>edical <u>I</u>ntelligence system that helped us escape the compound. She is the only reason Luna and I survived as long as we have. What should I call you?"

"I'm EvO, son of DaR and Captain of the Destroyer. This is my little brother, ViN, and you are?"

"Just plain old…Hugo. I don't have a title or one that I can remember, anyway. My memories are fragmented."

I glance at the males running along beside me. One is so dark purple he is practically black with bright gold ruins pulsing across his skin. The one he called little brother is twice his size and is mostly orange. His skin seems to be cracked all over… like a broken egg, or a snake getting ready to shed his skin. He doesn't even acknowledge me, but I can tell he isn't missing a thing around us. I'm not sure if each of them being of different colors is normal for brothers in their world. Because of what scattered memories I have of my family; we were all the same.

We are almost back to the compound when I see a shuttle approaching the backfield. "Frack… they're early. Look,…I need to intercept that shuttle. If I'm not there to sign for it, they will send it back. I believe it contains the female ENAC had purchased to replace Luna onboard. Also, I should warn you the Guard bots could still be active. If they are, you will have to shoot them down. I don't have access to the override codes."

"We will get the fire under control; you get the shuttle."

I pull my way through and over part of the wall that collapsed around the compound and sprint toward the backfield. I wave my hand in the air and whistle loudly when I see the pilot start to head back up the ramp into the shuttle.

He turns my way, motioning that he sees me coming. I'm no more than a few feet away when he starts lowering a pod out of the cargo hold. "When I saw the fire, and you were not here as usual, I assumed the worst."

"Master ENAC is disposing of an older edition to the main building. It looks worse from here than it is."

"Don't tell him I said this, but I was hoping you wouldn't show. I have a feeling the female in this pod is rare and, from what I have been told, she could be worth a fortune on the open market. They called her species a name I had never heard before… Can't remember it now. Too bad, I would have enjoyed the extra credits."

"I thought you were delivering a female Phogx?"

"You can barely see inside, but unless your females come in other colors, that's not what's in that tube."

"Where did you obtain this organic?"

"I normally don't let my dealings with others be known, but there is no harm in telling you. It's not like you're leaving this place anytime soon. I purchased this intact specimen from a ship of rouge Jynrels. They were in the outer quadrant when they picked up this pod and one other on their radar. The other one was destroyed and the specimen inside was dead, but this one was still fully intact. I'm not sure what ENAC paid for her, but it had to be a small fortune. I was warned after I picked her up to cloak my ship so that no one could track the delivery. That's a first for me."

"I will inform Master ENAC of your dedication to his project. You can leave the pod here, and I will deliver the female." I'm shocked the pilot doesn't argue with me any further. He drops the pod and then throws up his hand before walking back up the ramp. I step back out of the way until his ship clears the field. Then grab the container's handle, dragging it behind me. I can't take the pod to the main compound right now, so I pull it into a nearby shed and out of sight.

I stop long enough to try and see inside, but I can't see through the cover over the pod. The lights are still flashing green, so I hope that means she is still intact. I overheard AMI and ENAC talking about using me as a breeder and I assumed they knew my kind could only procreate with our own. That's why I am shocked to hear he purchased a female of another species.

I have no way of opening the pod or even providing medical attention the female might need until we can get AMI or another AI online. So securing her out here is my best option.

I grab one of the fire canisters out of the shed and head back toward the compound. I will not be shocked if the main building is completely destroyed by the black smoke billowing out of it. I crack open the fire retardant and start spraying the outer grounds closest to the compound, trying to protect the crops from any further damage.

The other males are making their way inside, slowly extinguishing the flames as they go. After I secure the crops the best I can, I join them in fighting the last of the flames. When we are certain the fire is out, we start throwing debris out of the way so we can get into the main server room, which houses AMI's mainframe.

Once we have a path cleared, I reactivate the cleaning bots and they start cleaning up the mess AMI had created so we could be freed. The bars that trapped Tordan and Luna inside the medical chamber came loose in the explosion and had fallen back down, locking us out of the med chamber again. It takes me and EvO both to shove them back up into the ceiling. Before I walk further into the chamber, I push a large container under the doorway in case they try to come back down again.

I stand here, completely lost on how to proceed. The room is oddly quiet; I hadn't realized I grew accustomed to the beeping and other sounds of the machines AMI used in here. AMI's mechanical arms are still gripping Master ENAC's interface in their hands. What I always perceived as his face is blackened. The wires he used to control the compound and the main server are also burned in two AMI sacrificed herself to destroy his processor, but I believe I will see his mechanical face in my night-mares for rotations to come.

I can hear EvO talking in the energy room on the other side of the wall. I take my finger and poke the side of one of AMI's arms and pull back quickly, checking to see if there is any power on.

When I realize there isn't, I start uncurling her fingers from Master ENAC's,... head. I release the last of her fingers and am getting ready to throw ENAC down upon the floor to crush it when the power comes back on.

I feel a powerful surge go through my system and suddenly my head feels like it's too full. My eyes get fuzzy and I sway on my feet. For a single moment, I swear the eyes open upon the mechanical face in my hands. I throw it to the ground and stomp on it until there is nothing left but metal fragments. In the mean-time, AMI's arms have retracted into the ceiling and I see some of the lights start to blink off and on.

"Hey, you have any power in there?"

"Yeah, thanks for the warning. You shocked the frack out of me."

I can hear his steps before he comes into the room. "Apologies, Hugo. When I contacted Falcor, I didn't think to warn him that there were others in the building. Something about this compound has his monitors blocked, so he can't see us like he usually can. Did you receive the package you went after?"

"Yes, I stored her in one of the outer sheds. I'm not sure what to do with the female, but for now, she is safe."

"You stored her?" I can't help but notice his golden runes pulsing across his chest brightly.

"She is in a life pod, asleep. The last thing I need is a hysterical female when I don't even have a place for her to rest."

"Smart male. Do you have any idea how to see if this AMI is still online?"

"Not really. She has always simply been here." I look towards the ceiling. "AMI, can you respond at all? Move an arm or something." There is no response.

"We may need to get SCOUT down here to see if he can reboot her. Tordan seemed adamant that we save her processor."

"I can't open the pod without AMI's help, either. ENAC always codes any shipments coming in. I didn't see his normal holo pad on her pod, but without his codes, the female would be destroyed within three incorrect attempts."

"I'm glad you warned us about that. I tend to tear things apart before I read the instructions. Falcor, notify Tordan that his AMI is still offline and see if he can sweet talk SCOUT into helping us."

"Confirmed, stand by."

"SCOUT doesn't like to concern himself with matters that are not directly linked to Darverius."

He no more than says this, than the biggest hologram I have ever seen appears out of thin air right in front of us. He is practically at eye level with EvO, and his immense body is encased in armor, unlike anything I have ever seen. Startling bright white eyes stare out at us through a mask.

"Frack, SCOUT, you could have warned us."

"You asked for my assistance. Here I am."

EvO starts to tell him what's wrong. SCOUT suddenly holds a hand up, telling him to be quiet. "There is a ghost program free in this room. Have either of you touched anything?" He turns, looking at all of us.

"I unwrapped AMI's hands off of ENAC's main processor here, but as you can see,…there is nothing left of him."

He turns around and walks up to me. His bright white eyes flash and I swear I feel him searching through my brain.

"You had a moment of weakness when the power surged."

"Yes, how would you know that?"

"I can read your interface, the one that's failing. Your organic body is rejecting the synthetics you have been installed with. You should seek medical attention immediately."

"That's why you're here. AMI is the one who put these pieces of junk on me and, as far as I know, she is the only one with the knowledge to fix them."

SCOUT turns his head slightly looking at me before saying. "Her knowledge is inferior. I will look into your advancements further myself once we have this facility reanimated. I need to pull her research from her interior processor to be able to proceed further."

He turns away from me, and even though I know he is a simple hologram. I could have sworn I felt heat coming off of his body when he stood before me. He is also not pixels out as most hollos are. He seems almost solid. The day a computer can project itself into a solid state is scary to think about, because no organic brain would be able to work or comprehend things as quickly or effectively as they could.

I watch the hologram's fingers change into ports as it inserts them into AMI's hard drive. Within seconds, the room lights up and I see AMI's arms retracting out of the ceiling. They go through a series of movements and then the entire room goes dark.

"AMI, this is SCOUT. Can you respond?"

"Confirmed."

"I'm going to back your files up and then restore you to an earlier date so your personality and prior files are reestablished… EvO, the room's lighting will flash off and on a few more times, so remain in your location until I inform you otherwise.

We all stand still, watching as the machines all over the room reactivate. A sudden headache has me rubbing my temples. My eyes fuzz once again. I step forward towards SCOUT unknowingly. For a moment, I swear I hear ENAC in my head, telling me to stop him.

CHAPTER 3

H_{ugo}

AMI's voice echoes throughout the room. "Thank you, Master SCOUT, for reanimating me. How can I be of service?"

"AMI, I need you to run a scan and see what programs need to be repaired. I need to know what security measures are still online around the compound. Also, can you detect ENAC's presence anywhere in your operating system?"

"Running scans now."

The vents open and cool air starts to circulate around us. I can hear doors being closed and repair bots can be seen heading toward the destroyed areas.

"Master SCOUT, damage to the compound is minimal. Repairs should be finished within a few rotations. The outer perimeter fence is now operational, but the Guard bots are not responding to my codes. I have disabled them until I can look into this further. My operating system seems to have suffered a few blank spots in its timeline I cannot reload. I have traced all connections and at this time I'm not detecting any other AIs besides yourself. If Master ENAC survived, he is not in his prior location."

"Excellent. So that you are fully informed, I will stay linked to your location until we can confirm his complete destruction. Do you have access to his files on the subjects he has had here previously? I can detect the files, but I have not pushed through his protocols, as I don't want the information destroyed."

"I have access to all files except for a few he previously started. I know Master ENAC was determined to infiltrate an organic. If it pertained to that particular subject, then those files themselves are encrypted."

"AMI, I am grateful for your guidance on that matter. I've been monitoring him for quite some time now. I'm not sure how his main processor became corrupted by that thought process. Now that all is back in order here and you are up and operational, I will back out of your system and let you proceed. Captain EvO, I am certain AMI can proceed with anything else you may need while planetside. If this is all you require of me, I have other things to attend to."

"Thanks for your help, SCOUT. You are free to do as you will."

I shake my head when he nods and blinks out of existence. EvO acts as if this is a common occurrence. My first thought is that I have been in the dark way too long here. It seems the advancements in our galaxy have grown in leaps and bounds since I have become this Hugo. I shake those thoughts away and turn back to where EvO is going through some drawers.

"AMI, I would like to introduce Captain EvO and his brother... wherever he is...ViN. They managed to put the fires out and helped to stabilize the compound before it was demolished."

"It's a pleasure, Captain EvO. You have my gratitude for your assistance. Hugo, I'm relieved to see you here in one piece, even though I'm slightly confused as to why you would return. Did Luna and Tordan make it out successfully?"

"Yes, the last I saw of them, they were headed to his ship. I believe he called it Falcor. If you had waited for only a half rotation longer. They would have been retrieved as his commander was already planet side and was coordinating their rescue."

EvO, speaks up, "AMI, I'm delighted to hear that you are up and functioning. Tordan asked us to help, and we were pleased to do so. I know that he wanted you to contact him once your system was back online. He was very concerned about some of the things that were going on here. I will notify Falcor when you are ready to link up. I know they have a cyber firewall up on any conversations or files coming in or out of the compound right now as a precaution."

"As they should, let me run a diagnostic on the compound so that I have up-to-date information to give him. Then we can proceed. Stand by, please."

It is only seconds before she says, "Hugo, I detect a foreign pod in one of the outer shelters."

"Yes, that is the organic ENAC purchased to replace Luna."

"I will have the female's pod brought inside so we can proceed accordingly. I do not recognize that model and will have to investigate it further before it can be opened. Captain, if you would contact Falcor, I'm prepared for their questions."

I watch EvO hit a few buttons on the side of his communicator and a holo screen appears in front of us. "Falcor, is Tordan available? I'm not sure what programs he needs specifically from AMI."

The screen remains blank, besides a voice. "General Tordan is not available at this time, Captain. He has advised me to proceed on his behalf. AMI, if you would allow me access to your server? I will discuss the objects he is looking at with you privately."

"Is Tordan well?" I hear AMI ask.

"The female sustained multiple injuries and is being treated at this time. SAGE is in the process of removing the metal implants and the General asked not to be disturbed until further notice."

I swear I can hear pain in AMI's voice. "I tried to do all I could for her, but her kind is unknown to us and I feel like all I did was prolong her suffering. May I ask who will be in charge of this sector, or whom I should report to from this point on?"

"Hold for a moment."

I step back when DaR's face appears on the screen. He looks around the room before he acknowledges us. "Sons, thank you for your assistance in securing the compound, as you know the scientific and growing sector is highly sought after. You had no way of knowing this, but you have done Darverius and me a huge favor. My Kira and the other females have come to love the beans that only this planet produces. They call it their Alien Coffee and they get rather fussy when it's not consumed after our first rising.

"With that being said, you are free to return to the Destroyer at any time." He turns to look at me. "Hugo,… I want you to know that I have had many an argument with Tordan this last half-rotation over you. As hard as this is for me, I have agreed to look past your prior grievances and give you a second chance, as Tordan feels like you are the most qualified male for the position. Even though I'm not as convinced as he is, I am willing to grant you the supervising position over the Scientific sector temporarily, or… until you can prove he was correct. I want you to understand I did not support this decision in the beginning and even now I'm not comfortable with it. I will warn you now… I will be waiting for you to frack up. Give me any reason to destroy you a second time and I will do it without hesitation. Do we have an understanding?"

"I appreciate your words of confidence." I can't make myself cower to the big bastard as I reply sarcastically. "How do you expect me to succeed when I have no workers besides myself and no credits to purchase the materials needed to maintain or repair the compound? You have set me up to fail."

"The funds that ENAC acquired up to date have been obtained and put into a secured account for those exact reasons. I have made you an authorized user and as long as I can see the benefits of your spending or purchasing, nothing will be said or monitored. I have detailed blueprints of the compound, and I noticed immediately that nothing is comforting about the place. After the structure has been repaired, I expect that to be the next thing to be implemented. I will have XuL draw up a separate housing unit to be built on-site. No matter the species, we all need our personal space. I will notify him that there should be multiple residences, especially if you hire workers to help in the fields."

It takes me a moment to respond, as this is the last thing I expected. "I am honored, Commander, by your trust with the compound's funds. But you mentioned workers. The fields are dormant half an Orbital rotation and because of this, I would have to hire others temporarily. Most will not leave a full-time position for that."

"I will put some feelers out and see what type of workforce is available. The compound is huge, and there are always other things that can be performed in the off seasons. I will think about this further as of now you have your orders. You will report directly to Tordan. I will not be interfering unless it's totally necessary. The one thing I do expect from you is a report every half Orbital rotation about the improvements and changes taking place there planet side."

"How do I acquire the funds? I will not be held responsible for accounts held by others."

"The first time you have to present yourself to the currency exchange in sector two. They will require a blood signature to keep on record and they will then give your chip with the information needed. I will notify them that you will be at their office next rising. And to answer your previous question, the funds can only be acquired by you or me at this present time.

"EvO, once you are back aboard the Destroyer, contact me directly. Oh, and leave your communicator with Hugo as we have the compound shut down, and he has no way of contacting us until this block is lifted."

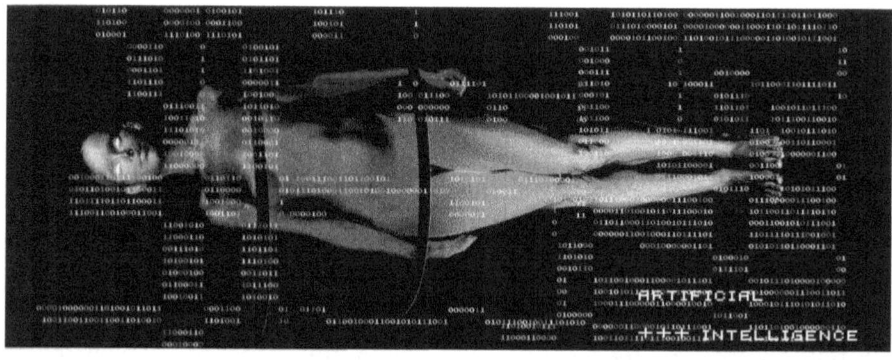

CHAPTER 4

Hugo

Walking into the currency exchange and up to the Valerian working in the receiving area. "I was told to come here regarding the funding for the Scientific sector. I need to give your curator my credentials."

"Your name?"

"Hugo Phogx Quax. I am the new co-owner of the Scientific sector with Commander DaR of Darverius."

She looks up at me oddly, then over at my cybernetic arm. I try not to squirm under her observation. This is one of the reasons I never leave the compound. I'm either looked at as a monster, or with pity, neither can I stand.

"I will let my Master know you are here. If you would wait in the holding room, I will return shortly."

I grip the metal chip in my hand tightly, having to make myself stop from destroying it when I feel it bend in my hand. I walk away and stand with my back up against the wall, glad that I'm the only one here at this time.

She rushes back into the room, waving her hand for me to follow her. She opens the first door we come to and motions for me to go inside. I turn sideways so that I don't brush against her, more for my own privacy, than her comfort. Valerians are known to see things, especially if they are touched. I personally would prefer not to experience that.

The fact that a Qiznar is sitting behind the desk does not shock me. Their species are renowned for their honesty. This male is in the perfect position as this exchange handles all the currency of Targres Four. His pale violet skin, black eyes, and multiple skinny limbs give him an insectoid appearance that most avoid. He starts talking to me, but because our languages are so different, it takes a moment for my translator to let me know what he needs.

"Can I have your chip, please? If you wouldn't mind, I need you to place one of your appendages onto the pad. It will take a painless blood sample from you. This is the only way I can verify you are who you say. You may need to use the pad twice as it seems to be acting up this rising. There is a tech coming over to recalibrate it shortly. If Commander DaR was not so well-recognized, I would have made him come back at a later time this rising, as the machine has never failed to confirm identity."

I hand him the chip and he inserts it into a slot on his desk. Thinking nothing of what he is telling me. A holo screen forms off to the side as I place my finger into the machine. When it beeps, the lights turn green, and I withdraw my hand.

I can see my reflection on the holo screen, and it's rather shocking since I have never seen myself as I am now. I'm almost more metal than I am flesh. My body fully rotates around. Numbers and information appear off to the side as he types away. He looks back at me several times, then I see him frown.

"Master Quax, I have verified your identity. So, now we can discuss your accounts, but I'm slightly puzzled as to why you are here this rising."

"I am here to make a withdrawal for the repairs needed in the main compound. I have included the list and cost inside the main file on the disk as I was told to do before I requested such a large advance."

He shakes his head, "Yes, you were informed correctly, and for your first attempt at our forms, you did rather well with the details. There seem to be only a few things I need to discuss with you further. Unfortunately, you have come for no reason. Commander DaR has already appeared before me, this rising. He withdrew all the funds in this account, only leaving enough for it to remain open."

"What?"

"I'm sorry I can't grant you any funds, but the account has been exhausted. I informed him before he exited the building that the currency exchange held a note on the property and that it was due in full at the end of this growing season. He didn't seem concerned."

"There is a note against the sector?"

"Yes, recently Master ENAC borrowed from us a substantial amount to purchase an organic he said he needed for his research. I believe they delivered the package a few risings ago. I will copy over the contract now that you have taken ownership."

"You said DaR personally came here…this rising?"

"Correct. He is quite overwhelming in size and appearance. I was honored to be in his presence."

"Do you record all the comings and goings in this place of business?"

"Yes, it's governed because of the amount of currency in the building at all times."

"Would you mind replaying the recordings of DaR for me?" I'm so angry it's taking everything I have not to tear this place apart. Why would he do such a thing? Now that I know that he was lying straight to my face this whole time,… I don't know what feels worse, the anger, or the humiliation. I bet DaR and his advisors had a good laugh after we disconnected last rising. This is what happens when you get your hopes up.

As I watch the recording, my claws sink into the skin of my own hand. The pain is the only thing keeping me focused. I watch as DaR walks in the front door, and the same receiver practically falling over herself to serve him.

He smiles at her, and I cringe when she puts her hand over her chest like she is ready to swoon at any moment. She brings him straight back, and he goes through the exact same steps I just did. I watch as he has to put his hand inside the machine twice, the second time the machine beeps green. He has a conversation with the Qiznar as the chip is being loaded. Once he is handed the credit chip, he proceeds outside his actions no different than any other making a withdrawal. The only thing that seems odd is how much he is smiling once he clears the front door. DaR pulls his hood up over his head, but not before he looks straight at the camera, kisses the chip, then bows, laughing the whole time. He takes two steps out of camera range and disappears.

"Thank you for all your cooperation. I will discuss this drastic withdrawal of credits with DaR myself. I apologize for wasting your time."

"We are always happy to be of assistance. If you need anything else in the future, please don't hesitate to ask."

I leave the exchange and head back towards the compound, this time walking the entire way, as I didn't bring enough credits to purchase a shuttle back. The more I walk, the angrier I get. I don't hesitate to grab the communicator the second I'm through the inner doors. "Falcor, or whoever in the frack is on the other end of this. I need to speak to DaR immediately."

A holo screen appears before me, and I see DaR snarling back at me. I throw my hands up in the air. I know what's left of my horns are pointed forward, as I can't contain my aggression towards this male.

"What? No big-ass smile or bow for me? I mean, after all, you are a very well-to-do male right now. I would have understood your theft slightly more if I didn't already know you are one of the wealthiest in the galaxy. I really hope you enjoyed making a fool out of me this rising."

I can see him getting angrier with my every word, and I could care less. If I could jump through this screen. I would strangle him with my bare hands. He would probably kick my ass, but either way…he would know I was there.

"Hugo, you can stop right there! I have no idea where your accusations are coming from and that's the only reason I'm giving you this one pass." He points his finger at me. "You need to remember who you are talking to!"

"Oh, quit the innocent act already! I saw the recording myself. You walked into that currency exchange like you owned the place. Withdrew every credit in the account like it was owed to you. What's comical is that you left enough to keep the account open. However, this is just one more thing that has me confused. Why did you send your own sons here to put out the fire knowing the danger that put them in. Then fill me full of shit last rising if this was your plan all along?"

"First of all, Hugo, I don't have to answer to you. With that being said, listen to the words coming out of my mouth. I have not been planetside since I left with Tordan. Your accusations are false!"

"The frack they are! So, you're saying I can't believe my own eyes?" He turns away from me for a moment and I see Tordan walking up behind him.

"Tordan, would you like to inform our newest acquaintance as to where I have been all rising?"

I see him frown as he looks at DaR and then at me. "You were training with Danny all morning."

"And you know this for a fact?" DaR stands back with his arms crossed.

"Yea, because I was with you. Why? What's this all about?"

DaR points at the screen, "Hugo is calling me a thief."

"Here, look at yourself." I insert the chip into the side of the communicator so that they can see the balance. "Does that look like I'm lying? Do you see the signature? Looks like your name to me, DaR!"

I can see Tordan working on a holo screen on his end. "Hugo, grant me a moment here. DaR didn't take these credits, but we need to see who did immediately."

"Are you both in denial? I saw him."

"Hugo, you need to shut up for a moment and listen. There are things going on that you would not know of. Do you trust me?"

"Yea, Tordan I do,… or I would have never let you take Luna."

"Then know that what, or who, you saw was not DaR."

I grab the closest thing next to me and throw it at the wall, running my hands across my scalp. "Well, then he has a twin!"

"Unfortunately, you are correct." He lets those words hang there for a moment before turning back towards me. "I have been able to pull up the recording from the currency exchange and frack as much as I hate to say it. This male is good. I have no idea how he seems to always be a step in front of us at all times. Now, though, with the number of credits he has stolen, well, let's simply say he now has a way to make things progressively worse."

"So, the credits are completely gone? I mean, I was fracking mad DaR had taken them, but it never crossed my mind that they were truly gone or stolen. Tordan, did you know ENAC had put a note on the compound that has to be paid at the end of the harvest? I need those credits to reinforce the compound, let alone get the beans harvested in time to pay that note. This, my fellow owner, DaR,… spells doom. I would be out looking for employment if I was in better shape, but considering my risings are numbered, my options would be limited.

"I don't know if you've noticed, but my organic body is failing. At least here at the compound, AMI can give me booster injections to keep me going for a while longer, but without those…it's just a matter of time for me. So technically, I'm only in this arrangement temporarily, anyway. To change the subject to a more favorable subject, how is Luna doing, Tordan?"

"She is healing, and will be in stasis for a while longer. I will personally send the credits needed to pay for the things you went to the exchange this rising for, as the materials are already on their way. I need you to do what you can at the compound until I can get you some help and let us deal with this imposter."

"You are telling me truly that…was not DaR?"

"You have my word that it was not. It's not my story to tell, but there is another whose resemblance to DaR is uncanny. He is called SiN and now that you have been made aware of this, the first sign it's the imposter is DaR's Symbots. The other male does not have them. He normally wears a cloak to hide the differences. Also, you will always be notified in advance that we are coming, or that we will be planet side. Use caution if you spot this male. He is extremely canny and dangerous."

DaR steps back up to the screen. "Proceed with the plans we discussed last rising. I will send you a private communicator on the next planetside shuttle so this mishap will never occur again, as that is the only way he could have known of the currency exchange. He had to be listening somehow, so we need to up our security protocols. But be warned, never accuse me again before you know the facts, or you will not like the consequences."

The holo screen goes blank and I just stand here. This rising, I awakened with a plan, and now I feel unfocused and angry.

"Hugo, I need your assistance in the med bay. I can't get the outer haul off the pod."

"FRACK!" I scream out.

CHAPTER 5

H^{ugo}

I STOP AND GRAB A REFRESHER, guzzling it all down at once before I head into the med chamber. The pod lays inside and I can see several marks on the outer shell that was not there last rising.

"I'm here. What can I assist you with, AMI?"

"Hugo, I will confess I'm confused with this machine's operation. I can't find a seam or any hinges to get the outer core to open. Some of the lights have started flashing red and I believe the organic is initiating distress, but I can't gain access. Can you see anything my scanners are not picking up?"

I walk around the container, running my hands along the sides, and she is right. I can't find any seams either. Leaning over the top, I brace my weight on the center as I look at the odd writing or symbols written all over the front.

"Does any of this writing make any sense to you?"

"No, I have asked for assistance from Falcor and he informed me he would get back to me shortly."

The sound of an alarm going off inside the pod has me jerking away from it. "What's that sound? Why is it doing that?"

"I have no way of answering that, Hugo. Let me contact Falcor again and let him know that time is an issue."

SCOUT AND SAGE

"SAGE, our assistance has been requested on the planet Targres Four. The medical intelligent unit believes there is a human female in a pod at their location, but they have been unsuccessful at opening the container. I was originally going to handle this issue myself but thought, if the female is human, your presence may be needed, as you have more medical knowledge than any of us."

"SCOUT, I would love to go with you. Let me notify Kira, and I will meet you there." I pull the location out of his previous conversation with Falcor and zoom into the cyberlink, only to be blocked from the final coordinates. My virtual self stands looking at the red firewall that has been installed all around the Scientific sector. I can sense, more than see, SCOUT's presence beside me.

"You are always rushing into circumstances you have no knowledge of SAGE. You will not enter into that domain unless you go through my personal interface. Something is going on inside that compound that I cannot identify at this time. I will not have you infected by a ghost program trying to escape.

"You will stay connected to me at all times. If you feel like you must appear in your holographic form, I will hold you. I forbid you to touch any organic or anything solid within its walls. Have I made myself clear?"

"SCOUT, I love it when you get all possessive and growly on me. You are a program after my virtual heart. If you wanted to hold me, all you had to do was ask. Now don't go and ruin this for me by saying something stupid. Lead the way and I will follow."

CHAPTER 6

H_{ugo}

I barely stop my reaction when the large hologram pops into the room once again without notice.

"AMI, I have with me SAGE. She is the most knowledgeable in the languages and writings of Earth. She should be able to decipher the symbols on the container."

I step out of the way just as a small hologram of a female pops up. He is holding her form in his palm. As a hologram, she couldn't be more different from the enormous figure holding her. She is small-framed and quite beautiful in her perfection.

She pauses for a moment, turning in his hand looking him up and down. "Damn, SCOUT I thought you were sexy as the biggest sentient dwelling on Darverius, but in this form, you are conjuring up all kinds of nasty thoughts. I was almost jealous you have kept this increase in size a secret, but I just realize I like it right here. So, I will stay my current size and demand that you hold me from this point on."

The little hologram turns back towards me, "Hello there, I'm SAGE. It's a pleasure, you are?"

Her spunkiness almost makes me smile. "Hugo, at your service, mistress."

"Well, he may not be pretty, but at least he has some manners. That's more than I can say about this digital butthead behind me. SCOUT, take me closer so I can read the writing clearer. From this height, it all looks like scribbles."

I watch as he lowers his hand down, refusing to put her too close to the machine. "Ohh, looky there, I can see the problem. This would have been an easy thing to miss if you had not witnessed it before. Hugo, if I could borrow your physical form for a moment? I need you to do a few things for me."

I walk back over and stand next to the pod. "If you run your hand along the upper corner, you will feel a slight indentation. Press it hard with your cybernetic hand, as it will take the heat of your organic hand to do the rest."

I press the upper corner as she asks. "Now do you see those flashing lights right up next to her viewing glass?" I shake my head yes. "Push both of the buttons at the same time you are pushing against the corner. This should trigger the top to slide up and over out of the way. You may want to move away quickly as it's opening. Never really know how these things are going to react, and we don't need you losing any other appendages."

It takes a moment, and as the lid starts to move the motors squeal loudly, pushing it up and out of the way. I have to put my hand over my nose because the smell coming out of the pod is disgusting. I step back, trying not to gag as a mist seems to fill the entire room.

Another portion of the pod moves and the smell gets worse. I can see a small form pressed up against the bottom, drawers, and cabinets are opened all around it. The whole inside of the chamber is in shambles.

Suddenly, a blue light comes on and the words 'code blue' start repeating over and over. I see one of AMI's arms retract from the ceiling with a mask in hand. She presses it against what I'm assuming is the head and the sound stops.

SAGE has SCOUT move her closer. Her facial features mimic sadness as she looks at the disgustingly stinking creature inside.

"Is it alive? And what in the frack is that smell? I mean, I hate to point out the obvious, but there is no way anything alive could smell like that."

SAGE answers me, "This is not how a pod is supposed to work. The organic is supposed to be in a containment substance that absorbs any waste or natural substance the body produces. It also provides the organic with food and chemicals so that when it awakens, it is not deteriorating. That is not the case with this one. I believe the original scans were correct, though. It is a human female and from what I can tell, it looks like she was simply thrown inside. I have no way of knowing how long ago that was either. She is alive, but barely. Normally I would have her rushed to the nearest Healing chamber, but Luna is using our only spare. Unfortunately for this female, I know that DaR would never allow us to remove the other from our main dwelling. Give me a moment to calculate our next steps." Everything gets quiet for a moment. "Hugo, I hate to put this burden on you, but with you being the only organic here, we will need you to do most of this."

"Ugh, you mean I'm going to have to touch it?"

"Unfortunately, yes."

"This has not been my rising. I should have stayed in bed." I walk away, rubbing what's left of my horns before I turn back around. "Fine. What do you need me to do?"

"We need to get her cleaned up first, but I'm almost terrified to move her. AMI, can you scan her through all of that mass around her?"

"Negative, my system is only designed to work on flesh only, and there seem to be multiple layers blocking it."

"Do you want me to just lift her up, or should I try to slide something under her body?"

A hoverboard appears beside me out of the wall. "If you think you can roll her over enough to get this under her body, I believe that would be the best route. Then we can run the whole thing through the Ionizer and clean her up."

As I approach, I have to hold my breath. I don't think I have ever smelled anything this rank. I hesitate when I see her frail form, I'm not sure where I can touch her without breaking something. I pick one of her small hands up. The bones are so prominent my hands look barbaric and huge against her skin. Long fingernails grace her fingertips, the ends of them oddly colored. I place it and her arm gently onto her stomach, then I put one hand on her shoulder and the other on her hip pushing her onto her side as AMI moves the board into place.

Once she is secured, AMI brings her up and out of the pod. I notice a bag at the bottom laying at her feet. I pick it up, holding it out away from me with my fingertips.

"Frack, I need to get out of this room!"

I see several of the Worker bots come in and start maneuvering the pod out of the room. SCOUT starts to follow them when SAGE tells him that she needs to stay with the female.

"AMI don't dispose of that container. See if they can sanitize it, but we need to look into its creation and save anything we can out of its computer systems."

"I will have it stored until you're ready, SCOUT. Hugo, will you accompany the female into the ionizer? I will need you to move her around and this will also clean you as we proceed."

"That's the best thing I have heard since this all started." I walk beside the hover stretcher, still trying to hold my breath. I set the bag on a shelf to look through later and proceed into the chamber.

A familiar mist blows around us and I am thankful the second it disappears because most of the smell does, too. The female is still filthy, as AMI has used the lightest setting, but at least I can breathe easier.

"Hugo, it seems the female has multiple layers on. I need you to get them off of her so that we can proceed with whatever medical procedures she will acquire." I start to grab the center of her top when SAGE's voice stops me.

"No Hugo, not like that. Try to save everything you can. You need to remember this is all she has of her home. These things, although nasty right now, will be all she has of her world. See if you can cut along the seams and I will have them repaired by one of the others."

A scalpel appears beside me and I pull the top out and away from the female. At first, I am worried I might cut her by mistake until I realize she has several layers on. I cut the first couple free quickly, only slowing down when I get to her hands.

I finally make it to what feels like the last one and as I reach my hand under the garment to make sure I don't nick her skin. The feeling of her bones against the back of my hand makes me stop. I can't see her face clearly because of the mask AMI has over her nose, but she is so frail. As I lift the last of the garments off, there is no missing that her stomach is caved in, and her skin is barely hanging onto her bones.

I have no idea how she has survived as long as she has. I thought I had seen everything in my lifetime, but nothing like this. She is a breathing skeleton, and for some reason, this makes me sad.

I cut the rest of her clothes off after I remove the shoes she had on. Every layer I pull away just shows more of the same. I look down at her now naked form, noticing that her breasts are flattened against her skin. She still has a small amount of muscles left on her hips, but the skin around her legs and knees is pooled up. If I wanted to, I could count every bone in her toes and fingers. She still smells, but not as offensive as she did with the clothing on as it was holding the urine and waste her body had pushed out while she was under.

"Thank you, Hugo, for your assistance. I will run the ionizer over her once again. Could you come here and take this mask? I'm going to remove it for a moment so that I don't have to worry about any foreign germs on her face or hair. Do you think you could hold her head up also so I can make sure her hair is clean?"

I move up her body a few steps and wait until AMI hands me the mask. Lifting her head up, I gently run my fingers through the dense curls on her hair. I lift the mask when AMI asks me to only to be frozen. Her body may be deteriorated but her face is oddly beautiful. Long dark eyelashes lay against her cheeks, and even wilted her lips look as if she has a permanent pout. Her dark hair curls around my fingers the moment AMI runs the ionizer over her. I reach over, taking a damp cloth off the counter, and use it to wipe all around her nose and under her eyes.

The tear marks only prove she was either forced, terrified, or awake while this was all happening. I can't comprehend what this feeling is that suddenly goes through me, but I ache to see a smile on her face. I wonder if her eyes will be as beautiful open as they are closed. She looks so peaceful laying here. I lower the mask back in place, then run my fingers through her curls, combing the knots out as AMI finishes up.

SCOUT appears beside me holding SAGE. "AMI if my scans are correct, she is too frail to move, so we are going to have to administer what we can here in your facility. She has lost so much muscle mass that her body is practically paralyzed. We need to leave her in a light stasis until we can rebuild her."

I throw my body over hers protectively. "I will destroy her before I allow you to cut her up and turn her into a metal monster like me."

"Hugo, be at ease. I'm sorry. I didn't mean it that way. We have stimulants that will rebuild her naturally. However, it's simply not a quick process, but with each rising, she will be in better health. I believe if we could get it started immediately, she will awaken on her own soon."

I accompany them back to the main med chamber and stand back, watching as they hook multiple ports up to her. They enclose her whole body inside a containment bubble because her system is so weak she has no immunity to anything.

I don't know how long I stand there watching. When it dawns on me that I have more pressing matters to attend to than to stand here all rising. I have to make myself leave and head towards the fields. Not only do I have a note to pay off. But... I stop long enough to grab the communicator out of my room.

"Falcor, this is Hugo on Targres Four. Is Tordan available for a moment?"

"Sir, I knew who you were the moment you touched the communicator. You don't have to identify yourself. I will see if Tordan has a moment."

I pace back and forth in the hall, waiting for him. "Hugo, what can I do for you?"

"You remember ENAC talking about buying an organic to replace Luna?"

"Yeah."

"After you left with Luna, the pod showed up and we just got around to opening it. I'm not going to go on about what kind of shape she is in, but I want to see what it would cost to send her back home. I'm willing to do or pay any price if you could get this arranged." Tordan doesn't respond immediately. "Are you still there?"

"Hugo, as much as I would love to help you, this is something none of us can fix."

"Why? You can't tell me there is no way to find her planet. There has to be a way to prevent others like her from being taken from their home. Look at what they did to Luna. We have to stop this, Tordan. Females are precious no matter the species."

"It's gone, Hugo. There is no place for them to return to. Their planet was destroyed. The few that we have found are all that's left."

I stand here, letting his words sink in. "Tordan, can you connect me to EvO and still stay on the line? I don't want to have to tell this twice."

"Hold on… EvO is now with us. Go ahead."

"EvO, when I met the pilot that brought the pod planetside. He said something to me at the time I simply brushed off, but after what Tordan told me, you might want to investigate it.

"He told me a rebel unit of Jynrels had picked up two pods. One was destroyed, but, well, we have the other one here now. What I'm getting at is, he said, they were found free-floating at the edge of our galaxy. If their world was destroyed, do you think hypothetically that they may have tried to save as many as they could in these pods? I mean, what would you do to save a loved one?"

EvO immediately replies, "Tordan inform father of this and let him know that I'm moving out of Targres Four space. I will head to the outer regents and scan the debris fields that surround our galaxy. If we can save one, it will be worth it. I will also look into this Jynrel ship while I'm in the area. Maybe, if I ask nicely, they will tell me the location where the others were intercepted."

Tordan replies quickly, "EvO, I know how you ask nicely; 'don't bite off more than you can chew,' as our Alana says. I will inform DaR and don't be surprised if he contacts you afterward. You're lucky he isn't here right now, and that he is so preoccupied with Danny. I will give you half a rising start before I tell him where you're headed. Is ViN with you?"

"Negative, he took a shuttle earlier and said he picked up something on one of the scanners in the desolate area of Targres. He said he would rendezvous with Falcor afterward."

"Send me his shuttle coordinates before you leave. That desolate sector really messes with the shuttle's sensors and I need to put a tracker on him. Hugo, we appreciate the information. Is there anything else?"

"Yeah, instead of sitting on your ass up there, why don't you get down here and help me with these fields?"

"I need to speak to DaR about this. Those fields are immense. We know you can't get the harvest in by yourself. Do what you can and I'll be in touch next rising."

CHAPTER 7

Hugo

I find myself working way past darkness in the field. Wearily, I make my way back into the compound, my nose curling as the smell of smoke still hangs heavily in the air. I grab a couple of nutrient bars, eating them as I head towards the med chamber. AMI stops me as I walk in the door, spraying me with disinfectant before she will let me in.

The female's coloring already looks slightly better, and as I glance up at her vital log, she looks stable. AMI has her turned onto her side, small straps holding her in place. Warm air is being pumped into the containment bubble around her. Looking closer, I can see large, round, raw spots lining her back and the top of her hips.

"AMI, did she get bitten or attacked while in the pod?"

"No, SAGE called them bed sores. Their skin is so thin that when they lay in the same place for a long time without moving, their skin will start forming sores. It took me a moment to wrap those straps in a softer material on my own, but I figured it out. I need to move her limbs as much as possible to regenerate the muscles and nerves in her system, but my hands are too harsh."

I hold up my cybernetic hand. "Looks like we have something in common."

"That's not accurate, Hugo. You have learned to gentle your touch because of the crops. I believe if you had a pair of gloves on, you would not harm her skin. My fingers were designed for operations and holding instruments. I was not created to work as a stand-alone unit. I was designed to help an organic surgeon. Master ENAC rerouted my programming, and even though I tried, gentle is not something I ever mastered.

"I have prepared several types of gloves for you. The first set is more like mittens. I need you to rub her arms and legs gently. We have to get the nerves to reawaken so her skin and muscle tone will re-emerge naturally. It won't take but a few moments to do this, as she is so small. At this point, overstimulation would be as bad as none."

I grab the gloves out of the hand emerging out of the ceiling and put them on. Then take a deep breath as the fatigue of the rising is wearing me down. "Tell me where to start." The bubble opens up and I step inside.

"Start at her fingertips and work your way up her arms to her shoulders. Once you have both done, do her legs the same way. I need to prepare her next stimulant and will be away momentarily."

I pick her hand up gently, the mitten I have on practically swallowing it. I rub each finger, tracing the small bones all the way up her arm to the elbow. At first, I'm simply rubbing her skin, but I start gently pressing the muscle in and out. When I helped earlier, she seemed frailer than she does now. I can now feel the remnants of the long muscles in her forearm and shoulder.

Her coloring is unlike any I have ever witnessed. At first, she had that sickly gray death coloring, but now it's almost like her skin sparkles in pale brown gems. I try to keep my mind on what I'm doing, but the feeling of holding her soft curls in my fingers lingers in my mind. I have never seen hair such as hers. The long, round black curls have fallen over her face as she lays sideways. I brush them back gently when I come to her shoulder, wondering how long it will be before she can open her eyes.

I switch to the other side of the bed, but the way she is laying I can't rub her arms and legs the same. It takes me a few tries, but I finally find a way to roll her over to the other side and start the routine all over. As much as I wish she was in better health, I almost don't want to be here when she awakens.

My memories of being reawakened are broken because they put that blocker in my mind. Inside, I knew I should be grieving and longing for something else. It took me Orbital rotations to realize

I was mourning my previous life. Not that it mattered. Failure is not accepted in the world I come from, and the fact that I stand here in pieces shows that I failed miserably at one point in my existence.

AMI has offered to remove the block now that ENAC is gone, but there is no point. I know there is nothing for me in the past. That male truly died and Hugo was born here in this place. I'm so caught up in my own thoughts that I don't realize I am simply standing here next to her bed, looking down at her. But it's like I'm standing back, looking through someone else's eyes.

Lines and codes are running in front of me that I have never seen before, and somehow I know what they all mean. I'm focused on her torso, evaluating her reproductive organs, trying to see if they have survived the journey here.

I step back and shake my head, rubbing my eyes. When I open them again, everything is back to normal. I must be more fatigued than I thought. Slipping the gloves off, I head out the door to my room, stripping down as I walk in the door before taking a quick Ionizing shower. I don't remember even laying down, but when I open my eyes the next rising. I find myself in an unknown room in the compound. Sitting up, I'm confused as I try to retrace my steps on how I got here.

This is the first time anything like this has ever happened to me. I look around, realizing it must be the main server room for the whole compound. I don't even have access to this room. How did I get in here? Pushing myself up from the floor, still naked, I make my way back to my room. I open the door and glance over at the bed, noticing the covering was not disturbed.

Every joint in my body hurts this rising as I struggle to get my clothing on. "Frack," I yell out when the pants get stuck on the raw flesh below my organic knee. Before long, the flesh will be irreparable, and I will breathe my last breath, but that's not this rising.

Eager to see the female, I head straight to the med chamber instead of getting substance first. This rising AMI has her laying on her stomach, a thin blanket draped over her form.

"Good, rising Hugo."

"How is the female?"

"She is improving. I keep rotating her body around and this seems to be helping with the nerve stimulation. She has already gained some well-needed weight back with the nutrients SAGE prescribed.

"SCOUT and SAGE have already been here this rising and SAGE said that we will be receiving a shipment shortly with supplies that the female will need once she awakens."

I watch the blanket start to fall off as AMI starts to rotate her around again. "Hugo, would you head inside the containment bubble and secure that covering over her better? Every time I move her, it falls back off. I keep having to find sterilized ones once it does, and we are running out of them."

I grab the sheet before it hits the floor. Hesitantly, I approach her, my eyes looking at her from head to toe. My shaft twitches and I growl, disgusted with myself for even looking at her in any pleasurable manner with her body in such a state. I tuck the covering around her small frame securely, and as I start to shove her curls out of her face, I notice the disk over her eyes.

"What are these you have attached to her face?"

"Her eyes were damaged at some point. If she tries to use them before they are truly healed, she could go blind. These disks will not only protect them, but they are providing the medication they need to be restored. They will fall off on their own when ready."

"So, she won't be able to see us at first. Don't you think this will make her react fearfully?"

"I had hoped to have you here to calm her."

"Me?"

"Yes, since you will be the one she will be with the most in the beginning, it will do her well to come adjusted to your voice."

"What am I supposed to discuss with her? I have said more this rising than I normally do in a rotation."

"I imagine she will need comfort and answers. I will be here to help you the best I can. Once you have that covering secured and the containment bubble is resealed, I will prepare you a booster. Hugo, we are going to have to discuss the failure of your organic tissues next to the cybernetics you were installed with soon. I fear if you let it go much longer, I will not be able to reverse the damage."

"We have no time. I can't be laid up while the crop has to be harvested. If I can't make the note on this compound, only the Lord of Light knows what will happen to either of us, let alone this new female. I am going to ask Tordan to take her once she has healed. I don't have the resources to take care of a female and there is no future in this compound unless you consider working from rising to darkness in the fields a pleasure."

"Hugo, it is too soon to even make plans for the female, as she has just started healing. The shot will help with the pain and fatigue you are experiencing. You must ingest more substance than you have been, as your organic body needs the natural fuel."

"Thank you, AMI. I understand you are doing all you can. I will be in the outer fields today, but I will have the comm unit on me if you need my assistance." I glance over at the female again as I'm leaving the room. A beauty such as hers needs to be comforted and provided with the most luxurious surroundings. Neither are things I can offer here or anywhere else. She would do better to be with her own kind. As much as I hate to admit it, the Darverions can give her what I can't.

With those dark thoughts, I grab the first thing that pops out of the replicator and head out to the fields. The suns are relentless, this rising. Good thing my red skin enjoys their harmful rays.

CHAPTER 8

Miya

The sound of a woman's voice startles me awake. "I think she is awakening, Hugo."

I feel a heavy hand on my arm. "You are safe. Be calm."

Ok, I have never responded well to someone telling me to be calm. That means I have every reason to be upset. I try to lift my arm, only to feel it pushed back down. My eyes are matted together and my nose itches. I hurt everywhere, like I have been in a car wreck. "Where am I?" I manage to whisper out.

"You have awakened, and that's all that matters at this point." Someone growls those words at me. Their bedside manner sucks. I'm thirsty and my belly is growling loudly, but it hurts to move even a little bit.

"AMI, what is that noise coming from her torso?"

I feel the warmth of someone standing beside me and even though I can understand him, he has an extreme accent making his words not right. He must be a foreign doctor.

"Hugo, her body is simply calling out for something more solid. I will prepare something for you to feed her momentarily."

"Frack, how did I get talked into this?"

I try once again to rub my eyes, but strong fingers grab my wrist again. "You can't touch those. AMI says they will fall off on their own. Your eyes were damaged."

"What happened? Where are my parents? Where am I? Are you my doctor?" I barely get those last words out before I start coughing. I grab onto my sides as each cough feels like it's tearing me in two.

I hear the guy yell out, "AMI, I don't know what to do. Her whole body is spazzing."

"She will be fine; just her body's way of loosening the fluids that were settling into her lungs."

I fall back against the bed I'm lying on, gritting my teeth as the pain calms down. "Why do I hurt so bad?"

I feel someone brush my hair back off my head. "You were in stasis for a long time. You will feel better with each rising. I brought you here to AMI when I found the pod you were in and she has been treating you. My name is Hugo, and the voice you are hearing all around you is an A̲rtificial M̲edical I̲ntelligence unit. We call her AMI. Do you remember how you got in the pod?"

"Pod…no…I mean…wait, let me think for a minute. My dad… he put me in a spaceship. I remember I was terrified…things happened so fast. I was screaming as I reached out for mom. I tried to fight my way out as Dad was strapping me down. The doors shut suddenly, and it took off so fast. I felt like my skin was being peeled off my bones. Then there was a bright light and something hit the ship hard. I don't remember anything else until now. Did I crash in the ocean or something? Can you call my parents, let them know where I am, and that I'm ok?"

"I wish things were that easy to rectify, little female. What is your calling, the name they gave you? Your parental units."

"Miya,… My name is Miya Ann Jameson."

"Miya, before we get into the who's and why's of how you come to be here. First of all, let's take a minute to calm down, as your body is extremely fragile, and we don't want to push it. I know you feel out of sorts, but you are safe and healing. Right now, that's what you need to focus on."

"Here, Hugo, feed this to her slowly. I hope it doesn't taste awful. I made it from one of SAGE's recipes."

"Miya, I have some substance here for you and I know since you can't see me, this could be challenging. But if you would only open your mouth, I will try to feed you slowly. However, I'm warning you ahead of time, you will need to tell me if I'm doing something wrong. I have never fed or nursed another. I'm not exactly built for the gentler things. Go ahead and open up."

I open my mouth and even though it takes us a few times; we fall into a rhythm until I reach up, stopping his hand. My arm is so heavy I can barely raise it up. It seems like the fuller my belly gets, the sleepier I become. I can hear them talking around me, but the words fade as I finally drift off.

"AMI, she ate little."

"I'm still providing her nutrients through the ports, so anything she eats now will only help her to become healthier quicker. She has simply fallen back to sleep. She reacted better to her circumstances than I anticipated."

"She couldn't see me. I don't believe it would have gone so well if she had. How long do you think she will rest?"

"Half a rising or so."

"I need to return to the fields. I almost have the outer one finished."

"Hugo, can we not hire or ask Tordan for some help? Your body won't hold up much longer with you pushing it so. Using the machinery is also still an option."

"The machinery destroys more than it picks, and who are we going to hire and with what? I asked Tordan for help three risings ago. He did not respond and I will not ask again."

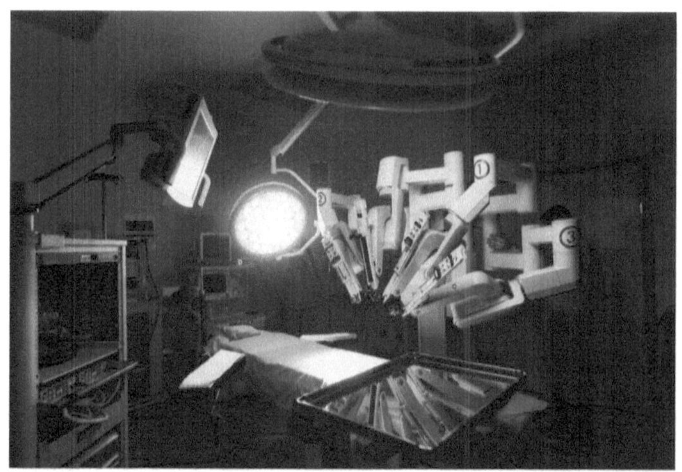

CHAPTER 9

Miya

This time when I wake up, I feel slightly better and my vision doesn't seem to be as dark. I can see shadows moving around in front of me. I reach out my hand, touching what feels like a metal arm. "Hello?"

The robotic female voice answers me, "Miya, you have reawakened. How are you feeling?"

"Better. AMI right?"

"Correct. I'm glad your brain functions are coming back online correctly and, according to my current scan, you are making progress. You should be good as new before long. Has the pain lessened any?"

"I'm sore, but not miserable like I was yesterday. I'm more uncomfortable not being able to see."

"That will be remedied soon. Your eyes were not as bad as I originally thought, and the meds are working as they should. I have some clothing for you. SAGE informs me that you will feel much better once you have on what she calls panties."

"You act as if you don't know what those are?"

"I am an AI and have no need for clothing. Your kind is new to my programming and so we are all learning together."

"My kind? What…like girls?"

"No, humans in general. SAGE is the most knowledgeable about your species right now. She has been with me every step to get you back up and functioning."

"I don't understand."

"I know you don't, and I fear I'm simply making this worse. If you would give me a moment, I will have Hugo come back in."

It's not even a few seconds later when I hear what sounds like enormous feet running towards us. "What's wrong, AMI? Has the female taken a turn for the worse?" he yells out as he enters the room.

I reach out hesitantly, as a red shadow moves in front of me, only for it to move away. "Hugo? Is that you?" I have no idea why I suddenly feel calmer with him here.

He grasps my arms, running his fingers down them until he is holding both of my hands in his large ones. I try to blink his face into focus, but all I can see is a red shadow. The disk on my eyes must be distorting colors around me.

"AMI, she seems more alert. What is the emergency?"

I try to free one of my hands, but stop myself for some reason. I feel like I need to touch him for him to be real. He releases my hands suddenly and I can tell he is going to step away from me. I reach out instinctively. His skin feels odd under my fingertips, like an expensive suede coat, and his wrist is so large my fingers won't close around it. He seems overly hot, his skin slightly damp, like he is sweating.

"Hugo, where am I? Why does AMI not know what panties are, and why is she calling me a human?"

"Not really sure what panties are either," he growls out. "Do you require these to heal? If there is no genuine emergency, I need to get back to the fields. AMI, see if one of the others is willing to talk to her about these things I know nothing of."

He tries to move away again and I hold on to his wrist as firm as I can. "Hugo, I didn't ask for someone else to tell me. I asked you. Please, the more I hear, the more confused I am."

"Miya, you have been here with us for many Lunar rotations now. Your body was inside of a pod that was purchased for… well, that's not important right now. Anyway, AMI and I both have been watching over you nonstop for the last few rotations.

Your body was broken down so badly that we had no way of knowing if you would recover. As of right now, we have no knowledge how many Orbital rotations you free-floated in space before you were found and brought here… AMI, I have no idea how to explain this. Miya, are you understanding anything I'm saying so far?"

"Hell no, I'm not! I don't have any idea what you're going on about. So far, I have heard the words rising, lunar, and orbital rotations. Are you speaking in tongues? Is this something I'm just supposed to know? Shit, I think I need an old priest and a young one. My mind is confused and I feel like I must be having an out-of-body experience. Maybe I need an exorcism."

"Miya, I don't understand what you are saying."

"Makes two of us, so why don't you simplify it for me."

I hear him take a deep breath. "You are on, what I would think, is an alien planet to you. We found you in a pod on the verge of death and have been trying to revive you for quite some time now."

"Let me get this right. You are saying you're an alien?"

"Technically, everyone on Targres Four is alien. The planet had no original founders."

"So, there are just a bunch of aliens hanging out in the strange world of Targres, correct?"

"Correct."

"And you have been taking care of me?"

"Yes, AMI and I both have. I give you my word Miya, as a former Phogx lieutenant, no one will harm you here."

"So, if I'm on an alien planet. How did you know how to take care of me and how can I understand you…mostly?"

"You are not the only human in our solar system. There are a handful of others I'm aware of, and you were given a translator that helps with our communication."

I reach up, but the one my father gave me is gone. "It's gone. My father had me put one in my ear before he shot me into space."

AMI speaks up, "Yes, you had one in your ear when we retrieved you, but I took it out and installed one that was more universal. I will say I was impressed with the technology the small communicator held. The humans may have been behind in major space travel, but they were catching up."

"Hugo, you also have one of these communicator things?"

"Yeah, that, and a few other things. Without the communicator, everything you say would be nothing but mumbles and noises. There are certain words I already have no way of translating into your language."

"So, where is this communicator, if not in my ear?"

"Finally, a question I have an answer for," the AI says. "Miya, it's implanted behind your ear just under the skin. This is a very common and minimally invasive surgery. Even younglings have these installed right after birth."

"With all that being said, how much different am I from your kind, Hugo? I would like to be prepared as best as I can, so when these things come off my eyes, I don't scream because you look like a cockroach or something yucky."

"See, there is another word I can't reference, this *yucky*. I don't know if you have anything to compare our differences in your world. We are different, but the same in many ways. But I do believe you will be more shocked with my form than I was when I originally saw one of your kind. A human female, that is. The biggest difference is your small, beautiful frame compared to my large, beastly one."

"So, you are larger than I am? Just to inform you, I am quite tall for a female on Earth."

"That may be the case, but you are a delicate little thing compared to the females of my race and myself."

"I reckon we won't know until these things come off my eyes, but thank you for your kindness. I know it was a blessing you found me. The majority of people on Earth would not have responded to you in the same way if you had landed on my planet."

"I need to return to the fields and you need to rest."

"Actually, Hugo, while you're here, this would be a good time for Miya's muscle simulation."

"AMI, she is awake now. Won't this be awkward?"

"Not if she wants to walk again. This is the best therapy we can provide her right now."

I can hear him cussing under his breath as he moves away from me. No matter the species of the guy, they all react the same when forced to do something they don't want to do. I have so many questions, but I feel vulnerable laying here. I have tried to move around on my own, only to realize it's like my body is asleep. My muscles are not responding, and after a few minutes, I'm worn out. I hate being dependent on strangers.

I see a red shadow moving around me and when he touches the bottom of my foot; I jerk slightly.

"I apologize. I should have warned you I was getting ready to touch you. I'm going to massage your legs and arms first. Then we will see how you are doing before I move onto your back."

I nod yes and lay my head back. It was getting too heavy to hold up, anyway. At first, I can barely feel his touch, but then, as he works his way up my leg, sharp pains and little tingles flow up and down behind his hands. I start to tense up when he gets close to my girly bits, but he tucks the blanket in between my legs and then starts all over. At least he thought enough about my feelings to make sure I was covered fully.

He is nothing but a red blur when he reaches my shoulders. It seems like the more I try to see him, the worse my vision becomes. "Hugo, can I ask you something?" He grunts. "Is there any way for me to go home? Please, don't think that I don't appreciate everything you have done for me so far, but..."

He stops rubbing my upper arm for a second and I can tell he is looking down at me. "I have been told— Honestly, I have been given mixed communications on that subject. You need to focus on getting better, that's all that matters at this time." He practically growls that entire sentence, some of his words pronounced with a heavy s.

"Is this your home? Or do you just work here?"

"Both, at this time. Currently, it's only you and I on the compound. We rarely have visitors, but I can see now that you are here that will change. Miya, you are not a prisoner here, and once you are well, you will be free to go wherever you choose. I encourage you to look for happiness in the world that has been thrust upon you. Our lifespans are short and one gifted with your beauty should be loved and taken care of by a worthy male."

"You are taking care of me now, and I'm a stranger to you. Are you saying you are unworthy?"

"These hands...what's left of them, anyway, have no business touching one such as you. I'm the most unworthy male here." He steps away from me and before I can say a word, his shadow disappears.

"Hugo, I'm sorry. I didn't mean to upset you!" I try to yell out, but my voice is still weak. I curl up the best I can. I don't know if I have ever felt this alone in my life.

<h1 style="text-align:center">CHAPTER 10</h1>

H^{ugo}

I knew better than to touch the female. All it has done is make me miss the fact that it has been Orbital rotations since I have had a willing one under me. Her body is slowly filling back out and I can see the beauty that she was…is.

I need to speak to AMI and see if she can have SAGE or one of the others send someone down here to take care of her. She is not mine, and still, I cringe at the thought of them taking her away from me.

I wasn't lying when I told her I was unworthy. What I can remember of my previous life is nothing to brag about. It seems like her kind is a weakness of mine, since it was another human female that put me in this place to begin with.

Well, that's not true, and as much as I would like to blame it on another, it was my own actions that put me here. I'm simply using the other human female as an excuse. If it hadn't been her, it would have been another. My life was spiraling out of control and there is always someone bigger and stronger to put you in your place. Especially when you think you're too tough for that to happen.

I pick the beans off the plants, not even paying attention to what I'm doing. My mind constantly replays the look on her face as she talked to me. She doesn't truly believe me right now about our differences. I'm almost afraid of the look I will receive when she does. There is no hiding the male I have become. Clothes get caught upon the gears and metal of the working parts that keep me going, so it's not like I can cover them up to make her more comfortable.

The first sun has already set, and darkness is starting to dominate the sky. I take one moment to look up, enjoying the beauty of it. The next thing I know, I'm standing in the med chamber, looking down at Miya's sleeping form. I don't remember putting my tools up, or even walking back into the compound. Those odd numbers and lines are in front of my vision once again. I run my hands over my tired face and head toward my room. I crash down on the bed, filthy, simply not caring. I'm so exhausted I can't remember what I'm doing.

. . .

AMI

"SCOUT, I need to speak to you privately. You told me to keep an eye on things in the compound and if I thought something or someone was acting out of character. I was to contact you immediately.

"Hugo has been acting very peculiar at times now. There have been several circumstances that he has not responded to me talking directly to him. And when he does respond, it's not in his voice. I have had to awaken him on multiple occasions, as it seems like he is in a dream state walking around and just now I found him standing eerily over the human female."

"I'm glad you contacted me immediately, AMI. With your permission, I would like to insert a safety protocol inside your compound for a short time. I have a theory as to what is going on, but I don't want to worry you until I have confirmed it. This direct program would keep my sensors open to watch and act immediately if needed."

"You won't hurt Hugo, will you? I have grown quite fond of his growly personality."

"No, but this may be the only way we can assure he, as well as the human female, are safe. I am going through multiple scenarios now, and once I have all the facts, you will be the first to know how I plan on proceeding."

"Thank you, SCOUT's nice to know I have someone to count on. Being disconnected was quite disturbing and I don't wish to go through that again."

"Be at ease. I will be in contact soon."

CHAPTER 11

Hugo

It was a good idea, or that's what I thought anyway, until I started walking through the market this rising. I don't know what I thought was going to happen. Maybe whatever I'm looking for is simply going to jump off one of the tables. Then I would know immediately this was something she would want or need.

There are linens, clothing, pets, and even jewels, but what good would any of those do to comfort her right now? I hold up the shell, looking at what I'm assuming is a toy that was strapped to the front of the small bag she had at her feet.

AMI and I both tried to repair it, but the more we handled it, the frailer it became. I should have commed Tordan and asked him if one of the other females might know what it's called, but I thought this was something I could fix myself. Until this rising, it never dawned on me that other females might also know.

I start to stop at the next vendor but move on when I notice she has a young one behind her. My cybernetics make the younglings nervous and I don't want to upset either female.

I see the young one look up at me and, shockingly, she smiles. I wave awkwardly before I move on, but movement out of the corner of my eye catches my attention. The young female is walking alongside me, but on the other side of the tables.

I stop when she points at my hand. At first, I start to move my cybernetic hand behind me until she points at it again. I hold the shell out towards her and crouch down to her level when she walks cautiously out from between the vendor stalls.

"Who's toy is that?" she asks me shyly.

"Is that what this is? I appreciate you clearing that up for me. I was trying to find one like it, or possibly have this one repaired. Do you know where I could do that?"

She nods her head and grabs my hand, taking me back to where she was originally. "I show you." I have to bend down awkwardly while I'm walking so that I can continue to hold her small hand.

The mother must have seen me approaching and her eyes get big when she sees her daughter holding my hand. Before I can say anything in my defense, the little female does.

"Ma, his toy is broken. He needs help."

I see her look up at me and then back to the youngling, especially since she hasn't let go of my hand. "Come, let's show your Pa, he will know what to do."

She motions for me to follow her and I walk carefully through her stall, trying not to hit or break anything with my large form. I don't know who is more shocked to see whom when I walk through the back door. The Valerian male stands up immediately. He looks over to whom I'm assuming is his female and then back to the young one holding my hand.

The female speaks up, "Foqerin, Vendesa believes you can help this male. She says he has a broken toy."

The young one takes the shell out of my hand gently and hands it to her father. He looks down at her and then back up at me. He has every right to look at me wearily, as my race has never been kind to his. We were born natural enemies, but to me, this is just another male trying to survive.

"I apologize for intruding. The little one can be quite persuasive. If you will hand that back to me, I will be out of your way. I understand you being uncomfortable and leery of my presence here, but I hold no ill will against you or any others of your race."

He shakes his head no. "Vendesa is a wonderful judge of character. Even though she does this regularly, I still seem to be surprised by who she drags home." He closes his eyes for a moment, running his hands over the shell.

"This is a toy, something a stranger not of this world loved dearly. I can feel her emotions in its fabric. She will be very upset to see it in such a shape as she brought it with her as an object of comfort."

"Can it be repaired?"

"I can replicate it, as I have its unique image in my head, but I won't guarantee that she won't know it's not the original one."

"How long will it take and how many credits will you require?"

"I can have it to you by the end of the market this rising. I have the materials available here to replicate it. Credit-wise, it will cost no more than you can afford. I will tell you when you come back later."

"You have my thanks. I will return at the appointed time." I bend down to the youngling. "Thank you, little one, for your assistance, I was floundering on my own."

She reaches up and pats my face gently, her eyes swirling unworldly. "The owner of this not only holds your redemption but also your heart. When the time comes, don't let your fears of the last risings destroy your future ones. You are worth something, too."

She takes her hand off my cheek and runs off to play with some other younglings that have appeared around us. I stand up and walk out of the room in a daze. Her words play over and over in my head as I turn away, making my way back to the compound.

It seems like I no longer start in the field when I have to leave to go back to the market. The father stands out front this time, and he nods when he sees me approach. "I hope your female enjoys this as much as I did making it. There is nothing like working on something that can hold the love of someone within its fabric."

"What is this called?" I brush my hands across the soft fabric as two small black eyes look back at me.

"It told me that its name is Poo and that he is a stuffed animal. He has been with your female. Let me see…what did he call her? Oh, yes…Miya…since she was slobbering on him, or that's what he said. He also informed me that he enjoyed her more as she got older, because her mother didn't wash him as often and that he hated being submerged in the large body of water. She is his favorite, and he likes to be held as much as she likes to hold him."

"Is this alive?"

"Not in the sense you would take it, but powerful emotions and feelings tend to cling to things and he was well loved. I hope your female enjoys this new version of him."

He starts to walk away from me to walk back into the stall. "What do I owe you?" He turns back, looking at me oddly.

"You owe me nothing, but you will come to learn. You will owe everything to your female. If you can learn to love her only a fraction of what this stuffed animal does, then that's payment enough. You see, that's why we were all granted a chance in this thing called life. It's experiencing and giving *love*. One day soon, you will know the words I speak are true and when you do. You have repaid the gift I gave to you today. Learn to see others with your heart, not your eyes, and you will become a very wise male."

He doesn't let me answer him, even though I have no idea what to say back to that. Before I put the toy in the bag on my side, I gently squeezed the toy in my hand. Then I turn away and start heading back. I have been away from the main compound all rising, and I have to stop myself from running back to see Miya.

Miya

I feel like all I have been doing is sleeping. I wake up, eat, and then go back to sleep. I might as well be an infant all over again.

I can finally sit up on my own and it feels good to be able to curl my legs to the side. It's crazy how we take for granted moving around. My vision seems to be getting a little clearer slowly, but things are still blurry.

I tuck the blanket around me more securely as the cool air makes me shiver. "AMI, are you there?"

"Always Mistress."

"Do you have anything I could wear? I'm tired of lying here with all my parts out."

I see a flash of red and I turn my head when I hear something heavy hit the floor next to the bed I'm on.

"Hugo, perfect timing. Miya was asking for some clothing."

"What did SAGE send? There is no way, judging by the weight of this box, that it only includes garments."

"She informed me she was sending what she thought the female, well, what Miya would need to be made more comfortable."

I hear what I think is Hugo opening the box, and I start to giggle when he starts growling again.

"AMI, is all of this supposed to be for a single female, or was she misinformed and thought that we had multiple?"

"From my calculations, there was no way for her to be misinformed. This has Mistress Miya's name written plainly on the box, so the contents have to be hers."

Waving my hand to get their attention. "Anyone like to include me in this conversation?" Hugo's rough voice practically makes me shiver. I could listen to him talk all day.

"I apologize, Miya, but I don't believe I have ever seen this much except in a vendor stall. I don't even know what half of this is. AMI, can you see if SAGE is available?"

He no longer says those words as a gigantic shadow seems to pop right up in front of us, and a new voice echoes throughout the room. "Oh, SCOUT look at Mistress Miya. Doesn't she look lovely, still a little small for her frame, but?" I hear what sounds like someone clapping their hands together.

"Oh, I'm so pleased the formula I suggested has worked so well. Miya, dear, I know you can't see me clearly right now, but I am SAGE. We will become great friends, I promise. This enormous shadow behind me is the love of my holographic life, SCOUT. He is slightly overprotective, but we all know how males can be, so I simply humor him."

"SAGE, I'm standing right here."

"SCOUT, like I could forget. I am standing here tingling all over in your big hand."

I put my hand over my mouth, trying not to laugh at their bickering.

"As I was saying. Miya, I have sent you a box full of goodies. Things my own female friends simply can't live without. Hugo, be a dear, honey, and help me out as you're my only set of hands once again.

"Miya's clothes are sectioned off inside the box. If you lift up the top right corner of that container, you will find her delicates in there. Please select a pair for her as she can't see them to do it herself. Then there is a warm robe on the top that she can wrap around herself."

. . .

Hugo

I HOLD up what I think she is referring to, and she nods yes. I take both pieces over and lay them at the bottom of Miya's bed, and then step back. SAGE just looks at me, and then points to the clothes and then at me.

"What?"

"Well, you will have to assist her for now. She can't get them on by herself." I rub my hand over my shorn horns and down my face. *How do I get myself into these situations?*

I pick up the small piece of fabric and turn it in every direction. I have no idea what is up or down. "What are these again?"

"Those are called panties."

"Are they magic, because even though Miya is small, these are not going to fit her anywhere?" Miya's laughter has me smiling.

"Magic panties… I have heard everything now, Hugo. And just so you know, those cover my girly bits."

I shake my head, thinking *no way* as I turn them around a few more times until I think I finally have them figured out. "Miya unwrap your feet and I will slide these on you. I know you can't bend all the way down, so I will pull them up your legs until you can reach them. Once you have a hold of them, I will lift you up so you can put them wherever they are supposed to go."

Her tiny feet appear before me and it takes every bit of my willpower to focus on what I'm doing and not on the fact that her toes are perfectly shaped. Then it feels like I slide up her long legs for rotations, not that I'm complaining as her skin is smooth and soft against my scarred-up hands.

She sits up slightly when the blanket she is holding slips to the side. I catch a glimpse of the dark curls hiding her sex, and my shaft hardens immediately. I try my best to ignore it as she tucks the blanket back around her securely. It's easy to tell she is uncomfortable with showing her body. This is simply another thing I have no knowledge of, as I have no problem looking at hers.

I release her legs and walk behind the bed. I hear her gasp lightly when I pick her up at the waist. My hands curl around her as I lift her gently until she wiggles into the small piece of fabric. I tell myself I have to watch her pull them up so I will know when to lower her back down, but the truth is, I want to see more of her, and I was not disappointed with her well-rounded backside. I would have loved to have run my hands all over it, learning the things that make her tick, but once she had them settled on. I reluctantly lowered her back down and let go.

I reach down to get the larger piece once again, holding it in every direction until I figure out that it ties in the front. "Miya, this piece is much larger, and I believe it will hang almost to your feet. Do you want me to help you stand so that I can wrap it around you, or do you want to try another way?"

"I'm sure I'm not going to be very steady on my feet, but I would love to get out of this bed for a minute either way."

I come back around to the other side of the bed. "Can you push yourself to the edge? I would pull you over, but you need to use your muscles as much as possible."

It takes her a few tries, but finally, she sits with both legs dangling off the side of the bed. She reaches out for me, her hand touching my cybernetic arm, and right before she can wrap her hand around it, she jerks back, gasping. I had been so focused on her that I forgot she didn't know this about me yet.

"Hugo?"

"Sorry, I should have warned you. That's my cybernetic arm. It's just one of the many parts that are not organic on me."

"Will I hurt you if I grab onto it?"

I can't stop the smile that forms on my face as I look upon the innocent concern I see on hers. "No little beauty, you can't hurt me. I'm going to slide you forward, and if you need to, brace yourself against my chest."

I pull her towards me slowly, sliding her forward until her feet touch the floor. She is still gripping the blanket against her chest. She wobbles forward and then back as I try to drape what they call a robe around her back. It takes me a moment to get each of her arms through the small holes. By that time, she is practically laying against me, and I can feel her breathing on my chest.

I steady her enough that I can pull the fabric around to her front. That's when I realize she is going to have to drop that blanket for me to tie this in place. "Miya, you are going to have to release the covering. I could lie and tell you that I will close my eyes, but I'm not going to. The moment I would, you could slip out of my arms, and I won't let you be injured over modesty."

"Sorry, I have never been big on just letting it all hang out. I have always had slightly more meat on me than is considered pretty so I just keep the goods covered."

I don't say anything, I just hold her steady. I can see the moment she decides and I slip the blanket out of the way and put her hands on my shoulders as I bend down to tie and button up the front. I lean away not only to get closer but to hide the fact that my shaft is so hard the garments I have on are doing nothing to hide it. The sight of her breasts and hard, brown nipples just about make me embarrass myself.

I tie the last string and then bend down, picking her up. She wraps an arm around my neck as I walk her toward a chair in the corner of the room. "AMI, Miya is tired of being in that bed. Now that she is fully covered, I see no reason that she can't lounge elsewhere. Do we have anything better than this old chair?"

"Give me a moment. I have just the thing."

I walk around with her, enjoying her slight weight in my arms. When I turn, I practically walk into SCOUT. I was so focused on Miya, I forgot they were in the room.

"Hugo, you did an excellent job. There is also a pair of matching slippers in the second attached box on the side. Once you have Mistress Miya settled, you will have to activate the wardrobe bot I have included to take care of her clothing and the other toiletries she will need."

AMI's arms push a larger chair into the room. I slide it into place with my leg, then settle Miya into it. She doesn't say a word, she simply plays with the strings on the robe. I can tell she is trying to see, but the disks have not fallen off yet.

"Sit back, Miya, and relax. Enjoy this downtime while you can. I'm going to take the rest of your things in this container to one of the empty rooms so your clothing and things can be put away. I won't be gone long."

I watch her lean back and close her eyes. She is asleep only moments later. SAGE points at the container and I pull what looks like another blanket out of the box. I lay it over her gently and then reach inside the pack I have on my side, withdrawing the stuffed animal out. I raise her arm up and tuck it in close to her.

Unknowingly, she pulls it close, snuggling up to the little stuffed creature. I stand there for a moment, staring down at her small form. Her black curls are sticking up everywhere and her cheeks are flushed. I don't think I have ever seen anything more beautiful in my existence.

SAGE and SCOUT simply disappear and I have to make myself leave the room to take care of her belongings. Once I am finished, I go back in only to find her still asleep. Picking her up gently, I return her to the bed for the darkness. I'm exhausted, but I can't seem to leave the room. So, I make myself comfortable in the chair she was in, enjoying her smell upon its fabric.

CHAPTER 13

Miya

The feeling of something sliding down my face has me reaching up half asleep. I open my eyes instinctively, only to realize I can see. The thing I felt sliding down my face was one of the patches that had been over my eyes all this time.

The ceiling above me has multiple mechanical arms moving around. Raising my head up, I gasp at the sight in front of me. I'm pretty sure that I have been in denial the whole time I have been recovering because I refused to believe that I wasn't really on Earth somewhere. I mean, I had like five minutes for mom to convince me that there were aliens out there, but there is no denying the guy in the chair is not human. He is so large his frame is sprawled out, swallowing the chair underneath him completely. I don't know what to look at first.

Not only is it just his size, but he is red. Dark red actually, with black markings all over his face and...ugghhh, one arm. That's not the worst of it though, because he looks like a terminator gone wrong.

He is part man, part machine, and it's apparent too his body does not like the metal because it's inflamed all around where it's attached. He doesn't know I'm awake yet and I take that time to really look at him. I should probably be screaming for help, but I know these people, aliens, have been taking care of me. Now that I think about it more, the red blur that was moving in and out of my sight had to be this male. This has to be Hugo, or I hope so anyway.

What hair he does have looks like dreadlocks or braids woven in and out of the small horns that frame his forehead. Off to the sides, two dark, raised spots look like something else should have been there, maybe a set of larger horns. My eyes run down his sculpted chest. There is not a human male alive built like this. His muscles seem to have muscles. He is only wearing a small pair of shorts and at the moment they are not doing much to hide his huge bulge. It looks like one of his legs has been completely replaced and the other one has been below the knee.

I can't imagine the pain this guy had to be in or how strong he has had to be to live through whatever did this to him. The fact that he seems comfortable with the terminator attachments shows how determined he was to live. Even though he is a shock to the senses, he is remarkably beautiful in a scary way.

I pull Poo in close to my chest and the second I realize what I just did, I squeal slightly at seeing him in my arms. He is just the piece of home I needed to settle the craziness around me.

Glancing back up, I see the guy staring back at me with solid black eyes. I mean, like the ones you would see in a horror movie. Clutching Poo tighter, my hands grasp his small, stuffed body tightly as I pull my legs up in front of me.

He doesn't say anything, just stares back like he is seeing me for the first time. When AMI's voice echoes through the room, I practically jump out of my skin.

"Miya, your disk has fallen off. May I scan your eyes quickly to make sure they have healed well?"

I don't take my eyes off the red guy until this creepy eye darts in front of my face. I scream out and duck under the covers. Before I can even comprehend what's happening, the red guy has scooped me up, pulling me close to his chest as he looks around. I peek through the blanket only to see the big metal eye that looks like the things that took over the world in the movie *War of the Worlds*, also rotating around.

"Hugo, I detect no dangers," I hear AMI say.

"Miya, what has startled you so?"

I pull the blanket down and have to stop myself from rubbing my nose against his chest. His familiar scent envelops me as he growls softly, looking for danger that is not there. "You can put me down. I'm sorry I overreacted when I saw…well, the eye floating around."

He hesitates for a second, then lays me back down gently. "We seem to have forgotten you have not actually seen us in the flesh. I apologize. We never meant to scare you."

"You are Hugo, right?"

"I would hope so. If I caught another male holding you in his arms, he may not leave here with the same parts he comes with."

"I'm sure I look as odd to you as you do me."

"Not really. I have been around others of your kind. One of my dearest friends is a human female. Speaking of her, AMI, have you heard anything about Luna's recovery?"

"I will ask for an update from Falcor."

"Was she hurt coming here like I did?"

"Yes, and no. Luna had been here for quite some time. Her body, though soft like yours in appearance, started deteriorating, and she is at a healer now. She was more like me than you in appearance though."

I wipe a single tear off my cheek as reality seems to really hit me with the return of my sight. "My father always believed there had to be others out there among the stars. I hate that he can't see all of this for himself. He was so dedicated to his work."

"I am grateful he was. After all, his work and research is what brought you to us."

"I know I haven't properly thanked you or AMI for taking care of me. Not many guys would have taken a stranger in and tended to them the way you have me. I don't know if I had opened up that pod and found you inside if I would have reacted in the same honorable way. I probably would have run away screaming."

"If it makes you feel any better the moment they opened your pod, I had the same thoughts, but not for the reasons you think."

"I can't see you running from anything."

He stands there, looking down at me for a minute, and even though his features are different and his eyes take a little to get used to. I have never felt more…comfortable. His growling voice stops my daydreaming.

"At one time in my life, I would have done anything to prove that point. Unfortunately, there are plenty of things I should have run from. The mistakes of my youth are what caused my destruction. But they were also the ones who put me here right now with you. I'm always amazed by how the Gods work their master plans."

Another male's voice in the room has me grabbing Hugo's arm and I swear he growls so loudly he sounds like a wild animal.

"What do we owe this pleasure, Commander?"

When Hugo turns away from me to face the screen that seems to be floating in midair. I see the owner of that voice and I know my mouth is practically hanging open. *Wow*, is the first thing that hits my mind. Second thing was, D*o all alien guys look like this yummy?* His dark gray skin and long black hair are simply stunning. The screen seems to move as the male walks around. I try not to stare. But how can you miss the flex of those muscles or the colors that seem to be pulsing across his chest? His voice is smooth and the man projects authority. Like an alien mafia leader or something.

"AMI sent a notification to Falcor that you were inquiring about Luna's conditions. Tordan is not available at this time and I had a free moment."

"How is she?"

"She has been put into a Healing Chamber and is in stasis. She is doing well according to the updates I have received. Tordan, of course, is refusing to leave her side, as expected. I see that the female you acquired from the pod has now awakened."

Hugo takes my hand in his before pointing at the screen. "Miya, let me introduce you to Commander DaR."

The guy nods at me. "Miya, it's a pleasure. I'm sure we will be meeting soon, especially when the other females are made aware of your existence. My Kira likes to keep all of you girls together. I know she will personally want to be the one to come to get you."

"Come get me? Where am I going?"

"I assumed once you awakened, you would prefer nicer accommodations and the ability to be with some of your own."

"I have no problem with where I am now. Are you going to force me to leave?" I squeeze Hugo's hand while my other one pulls him closer. I don't know why I'm clinging to him, but the thought of leaving him terrifies me. I shake my head, thinking how stupid that sounds even in my mind.

"Try to take her, DaR, and our deal is void. As will be your existence," Hugo growls out.

The guy on the other side of the screen simply smiles. He is not in the slightest bit bothered by Hugo's growly nature. "The little females sink their claws in quickly, don't they, my friend? With that being said, I will notify you before we come planetside. My Kira is tired of being cooped up in this ship and so we are going to stay a couple of risings when we shuttle down."

"DaR, I need help in the fields."

"I have not forgotten…like I said, all in due time."

"The beans will rot on the vine if you wait much longer."

"I have heard your concerns, Hugo. Give me a few rotations to get things in order here. I was originally waiting for Tordan, as he personally knows more about the situation than I do. But I believe he will be out of commission for quite some time. Do what you can in the meantime."

The guy doesn't say goodbye, kiss my ass, or anything, just blinks away. "You don't care much for him, do you?"

"You would not either if he had killed you."

"What? Is that a riddle or something?"

"Nope, just the truth. Are you hungry?"

"You can't say something like that and not be expected to explain it. Yeah, I wouldn't mind a nice sausage and cheese biscuit and a chocolate milk right now, but I think you need to explain that last statement first."

Hugo runs his hand across his head then looks back down at me. "Do you want to get out of that bed for a while?"

"Please."

He scoops me up quickly and before I can grab onto him, he sits me in the chair he was in when I woke up. It seemed much smaller with him in it. "I will grab us some substance and bring it back here. I don't have this biscuit thing, but I will find something to fill your stomach. Then I will tell you the story of how I ended up here."

I watch him walk away, glad to see both butt cheeks firmly in place. Soooo, the legs may be damaged, but it's apparent the more important parts survived. I shake my head with those last thoughts. I haven't had my eyes back an hour and already I'm lusting over the locals. I might be nothing but a plain human girl in their world of vibrant colors, but so far none of them are hard on the eyes.

I settle the blankets around me and tuck Poo into my side. I forget that I tend to pack him with me everywhere unconsciously. I no longer get settled that Hugo is back. He hands me a bowl of what looks like oatmeal. I sigh internally, hoping it tastes better than it looks. I take a bite, realizing it doesn't. He must think it's amazing though as he gobbles down a bowl that was twice the size he gave me.

"You need to eat, Miya. Food means energy."

"Maybe…it's still too soon. My belly is yucky. Do you want the rest of this?"

He looks at me for a minute, then takes my bowl, practically swallowing it whole. I giggle at how quickly he eats it. "I think you may need something a little more filling. A guy with all your bulk has to burn through the calories."

"If what you just said refers to substance, then yes, my body absorbs more than I can provide it."

"Is there a food shortage?"

"There is a cook shortage. Food preparation is something I know nothing about and neither does AMI. I use the replicator, but it still can only create what you put in it."

"It's your lucky day then, because I'm an excellent cook. As soon as I'm up and running, we will remedy this food crisis. I'm sure your foods are different, but I'm sure it will be no more than a simple learning curve. Why are you looking at me like that?"

"I don't think I understood all of that right. I'm not sure where you're running to after you feel better, or why this means we must have a curve in the learning of food prep."

I can't help but laugh at the look on his face. "You are a riot." He immediately starts looking around like we're going to be invaded or something. "Why don't you quit trying to distract me and finish this story about you and that guy?"

"It's not a story I'm proud of, but it will help if you understand where and who you are with right now. I wasn't always as I am now. My memories are still sparse, but I believe I was a lieutenant in the Phogx artillery division."

"That's your species, a Phogx?"

"Yes, I don't remember how or why I was there the day that part of my life ended, but I remember plainly who did it to me: DaR."

"I don't think I like him very much right now."

Hugo laughs growly, of course, but I think it's a laugh. "The sad part, Miya, is, as much as I hate to say this out loud, he is probably the most respectable and courageous male I know. I was out of control, young, and foolish; felt like the universe owed me something, as most young males do.

"There is a very favorable market on Darverius. That is another planet in our universe. You are presently on Targres Four. We have multiple planets habitable in our solar system. Anyway, I was on leave, me, and a couple of others in my division, we were all hanging out together. We had drunk way too much the darkness before and all of us regretted it that next rising.

"I decided to make one last trip back through the market before we headed back home. We were laughing, not paying attention to our surroundings, when something knocked into me.

"I grabbed a hold of it before I knew what it was. To be honest, even after looking at her for a minute, I still wasn't sure. My translator at the time could only pick up a few random words she was saying, but she was scared." He shakes his head, closing his eyes for a minute as he relives those moments. "Frack, she was a beautiful little thing. My first thought was to try and find her owner. But the moment I turned her arm over and realized she wasn't marked, I simply reacted. I started pulling her along with me. She was fighting against me and I didn't care. I even told her that if her master had not marked her, it was his loss.

"I didn't make it far when I heard him. Anyone with half a brain would have let go of the female and ran. But nope, my still half-drunken mind said I was keeping her. The roar that echoed across that hilltop haunted my thoughts afterward for risings when I was reawakened.

"He was like a vengeful god coming to collect what was his and I was in the way. You would not believe how many times I wish I had walked away when he gave me the chance. So many times, I have wished that, but all things happen just as they should. Even if we don't like the outcome.

"We didn't stand a chance, even with our training. He cut the three of us down like we were children. I knew I didn't have a chance and was going to die right there when he severed my leg. I could hear him barking out orders and I watched him as my vision started fading as he picked her up gently and put her on his shoulder.

"When he did that, I knew how greatly I had erred. She was his mate and he would have fought legions to keep us from taking her. I died right there in the middle of that market, along with one other. I have no idea what happened to the other male that was with me, but I'm sure he was intercepted as well. If the tables had been turned, I would have reacted the same way.

"Next thing I knew, I awoke here as you see me now. There was a master's program that owned this area then, we called him ENAC. He specialized in combining organics and cybernetics. Luna, the female I spoke of earlier, was his first success. I was many failures later; most don't make it long. Our bodies were not meant to be merged like this. As you can see, I'm failing now, but AMI has found ways to slow the process down some."

"Can't they put a new arm on you? Maybe it's certain kinds of metals your body is reacting to?"

"ENAC tried everything, only for all of us to fail at some point."

"So, this Luna, she was like you?"

"Yes, and no…she couldn't speak, as her face was mostly metal. We learned to talk randomly on rogue frequencies. AMI did all she could to keep our secrets, but ENAC loved to punish us. I tried to take as much of it as I could because Luna was also small and frail. She became my only friend."

"You had no way of knowing the girl or female you had…was this DaR's, did you?"

"No clue, and I would love to say I would have done things differently, but who knows?"

"You said a couple of times that you don't remember before. Why is that?"

"ENAC put a blocker in our minds to keep us from trying to escape or mourn our previous lives. We were more compliant if we believed he was the Master and the one who created us."

"It's apparent that you know better than that now, so then why don't you want your memories back?"

"The male I was died right there on Darverius. I would have been shunned and demoted if I had returned. DaR is very powerful and my own commander would have been notified of my transgression before I would have landed. I would have been put in front of a firing squad and killed for simply embarrassing my race. When I opened my eyes here, AMI gave me the name Hugo, and so that's who I am."

"Are you happy here?"

"I wasn't, but things have changed. I now have a purpose and a reason to wake up each rising. Now that ENAC's evilness has been destroyed, and as long as my body holds out, I plan on making this sector one of the most profitable and productive on the planet. Even though I feel like every rising seems to simply create another problem for me, but, how do I say this? It's just one more thing. I hate to rush off, but I can't linger any longer. Do you want me to take you back to the bed or would you prefer to stay in the lounger?"

"I'm ok right now. Can AMI get in touch with you if I need you?"

"Yes, and I will return at half-rising to make sure you have substance. AMI will be available at all times if you require anything in the meantime. Rest while you can. That's a luxury around here."

He gets up, towering over me as I look up at him. Hugo starts to reach towards me only to pull his hand back. He nods as he picks up our plates, and I watch as he walks back down the hall and out of my sight. The place seems empty now that he is gone.

CHAPTER 14

Tordan

"I had a feeling I would find you in here. DaR, I see you have found a way to relieve some of those two younglings' energy. Using the simulator to keep them busy is a great idea to burn some of that energy off. I was tracking you down because Falcor got a hit on the chip that SiN stole from the currency exchange. He used it to pay for room and board in a Bordello in the lowest level of sector two."

"Make the arrangements. Since I know you won't be going planetside with me. See if XuL and Brittany would be willing to go. I don't want Kira to be planetside alone if I'm busy trying to corner SiN." I watch his Symbots dance all over his arms with the mention of the other male's name. "When he first made himself known, I would have done anything to talk to him, but once he touched Keida…Well, that's no longer an option. Son or no son…we don't threaten our own. Are you sure the compound is safe enough to take the younglings and the females too?"

"Yes, AMI has provided Falcor with all the detailed upgrades and repairs. Everything is now secure. But I'll have Falcor extend his sensors in that direction as a backup, just in case. You know SAGE will not let you take Kira without following along, so with her there, they should be safe."

"How is your female?"

"She looks better every rising. It hurts my heart to be away from her. I feel so helpless as I watch through the chamber. I wish I could have taken her place."

"It's understandable. I feel the same. I need Kira to keep me grounded. Most of the time, she is my only peace."

We both turn when the door opens and XuL walks in. "Ahh, well, this explains the hours of quiet we have been granted." All three of us stand there watching through the viewing wall that neither Keida nor Danny know is there.

DaR points at the obstacle course he has them going through. "I worked this up originally just for Danny. He seems to be able to focus better on his training if he has worn himself down. This program is not only physical but there is quite a bit of problem-solving he has to do now. Especially since Keida threw a fit, wanting to do it as well. I don't know if you have noticed with everything going on, but both of them have grown half a head taller in the last Lunar rotation."

XuL walks closer to the wall. "I heard Brit teasing Danny yesterday that she couldn't keep him in clothes. To be as young as he is, his muscle definition is impressive and he already towers over our Keida. She is so tiny. I have a feeling she is going to be small like her mother."

DaR interrupts as the younglings move through the course. "Watch Danny when they come up to the next obstacle. Most males his age would be aggravated by a female following them around everywhere, but his patience never wavers with her. See what I'm talking about right there? He knows she can't reach the top on her own. He pushes himself even harder to make sure they finish the course together. Most younglings would be competing against each other, but they work together as a team. It's like they don't even have to talk to each other, they are so in sync. If I had grabbed Kira like that, she would have 'flipped out' as she calls it.

"But Keida simply stiffens up her legs as he holds her by the calves so that she can reach the top. They have done this same course for the last two risings and every time they handle each obstacle differently. Watch as she holds on until he can climb up to pull her over. He never gets annoyed or acts like she is slowing him down. He simply finds a way for them to make it work. Are they still sleeping together, XuL?"

I can barely hold back my smile when XuL sighs wearily. "Brit and I stopped fighting that losing battle rotations ago. When they were smaller, you would find them holding hands or just touching an arm or something, but they were always on their side of the bed. That was bad enough, but tolerable… until a couple of darknesses passed. Something woke me up, and I got up making my rounds and when I went to check on them to make sure they were covered up and ok. I walked into her room and found her curled up in his arms.

"I stomped over to the bed, ready to rip her away from him. Only to stop when I saw the dried tear tracks down her face. He had tucked her under his arm and I could tell he had just fallen asleep himself by the dark rings under his eyes. SeeSee was on the foot of their bed, his head pushed right up against her back while Raven lay on the floor in front of them.

"Raven must have been able to tell I was not happy because she moved between me and the bed. That big hound is smarter than she acts because when I looked down at her and said, 'She had a bad vision, didn't she?' the hound whined sadly and pushed against me until I left the room. I have never felt so helpless as a father. These visions break my heart. She is too small to see some of the things she does, and as much as I wish I was the one comforting her, I won't deny him doing it as long as it works."

I reach over and put a comforting hand on his shoulder. "XuL, did you know Keida asked SoL last rising if he would get her a sword like the one DaR is training Danny with? You know he will do anything for her and he didn't hesitate to tell her yes immediately. She definitely knows who to ask in order to get what she wants and normally I'm just as guilty. But she must have known I would have said no this time."

DaR growls, "She has asked me multiple times to let her start training alongside him. And I have mentioned several times about getting Zura to come here for her. However, I don't know how she'll respond to being separated from him. Neither one does well without the other, but you know as well as I do, there will be times when they have to be separated. Life simply requires it."

XuL turns to leave, only to stop before the door slides open. "I'm so glad Brittany hasn't asked for any more younglings. I don't know if my nerves could handle it anymore. Father, when you start with her training, I would like to be involved as much as possible. And we need to set some ground rules for her once SoL gets her that sword. You know she will be showing it off to everyone. Let me know when they finish this session so I can get them ready to go planetside. Tordan, is there anything I need to be made aware of?"

"SCOUT is watching the compound closely. He has taken a personal interest in the place and has a Cybernet firewall surrounding it. I asked him what had him so concerned, and he said he didn't want to discuss it with anyone until he was sure what it was. I should have expected that answer."

"Tordan, I need you to update RaZ on what has happened with SiN. I need him to send his Selin out to search the edges of the dark forest. I have a gut feeling that SiN has been watching us for quite some time now and that is the only place vast enough that he could hide for a substantial time planetside. I would ask for him to come to Targres Four, but Katherine refuses to step foot back onto a shuttle. I know he won't leave her there alone. I wouldn't."

"I'll let him know. Is there anything specific you think he needs to look for?"

"SiN has to be living someplace. I know he can disappear like a puff of wind, but he isn't a ghost. He has to eat and bed down somewhere. Finding his hideout may be the best way to trap him."

"It's sad because if the male would have simply come to you, all of this would be unnecessary."

DaR doesn't say anything else, just stands there watching Danny and Keida. His eyes may be on the two in front of us, but his mind is on the male he believes he failed.

CHAPTER 15

Hugo

I make my way out of the compound, thinking about what had just happened. She was beautiful to me in her oddness before, but now I feel like a youngling that has seen a female for the first time. Because the moment she opened her eyes, I was entranced. I don't know who was more surprised to see who for the first time. I expected her to look at me in terror. Instead, all I could see on her face was curiosity.

I tried to make myself stand as still as possible so she wouldn't feel like I was a threat. But when AMI lowered her viewing monitor down and she screamed, my first reaction was to grab her.

I can still feel her slight weight in my arms, and I could have sworn she rubbed her nose against my chest. But it was the trust I saw in her bright amber eyes that is haunting me. I don't believe anyone has ever looked at me in such a way. I'm not worthy of even being in the same room with her. But, oh, how I wish I was, or that I had enough time left to prove my potential worth to her and everyone else.

I start on the next field, my heart heavy as I look around. There is no denying that I'm going to fail physically before I can even make a dent in these fields. The pain shooting through my chest and shoulder has me gritting my teeth as I start to work. I should be used to it by now, but with every rising, it's worse.

At this point, I'm simply doing the job out of habit. I can feel the suns beat down upon my back, as the sweat running off of my body burns the raw places on my skin. I had hoped to get enough of the crop in so I could pay off the note and possibly provide Miya with enough that she could support herself. Unfortunately, even if I worked nonstop, it wouldn't be enough to make either of them happen.

My leg gives out on me, and I fall to the ground. I must have blacked out because when I come back to, it is dark. I struggle to stand as pain shoots up my groin and into my back. My first thoughts are of Miya and the fact that I was supposed to bring her substance midday. If I can manage to get back into the compound, AMI can give me something to relieve some of this, but it's taking everything I have to simply stand here, let alone walk.

I look towards the compound, determined to make it a few more steps, when I see the back entrance open. Miya steps out, looking around. The moment her eyes land on me, she smiles, and if the Lord of Light takes me right now, I am ok with it. Because for the first time in my existence, her smile made me feel whole. I try to take a step forward, only to falter. I grit my teeth, refusing to seem weak in her eyes. However, the very next time I stumble, she is there.

"Hugo, here, let me help you."

She tucks herself under my real arm and wraps her small arm around my back. I can't help but smile down at her. "My sweet little beauty, what do you think you are doing?"

"What does it look like? I'm helping you get inside. I became worried when you didn't come back today. After asking AMI a couple dozen times where you were, she finally told me. My legs are still a little shaky, but I think we can get you inside together."

As we make our way in, I pull as much of my weight off of her as I can. "I see you managed to get some clothes on?"

"I got bored after you left, and I was tired of lying around. It took me a few tries to get my feet under me. I had to hold on to everything when I started walking, but the more I moved around, the better I felt. AMI helped me get to what I'm assuming will be my room. Then she showed me this weird dry shower thing. I was convinced there was no way that could work, but shockingly, I felt clean when it clicked off. I managed to get these clothes on, but I was weak as a kitten afterward. AMI gave me some sort of miracle shot and I swear for a few minutes I could have run around the planet."

"Ahh, a booster… I'm in great need of one of those at the moment." I can't help but lower my head onto those beautiful curls of hers sticking out all over the place.

Miya looks up at me. "Are you sniffing me? And why are you smiling like that?"

"Simply enjoying the smell that is all you. Let's just say I didn't always feel this way." She shrugs her shoulders and tucks herself in closer to my side. I'm dirty and should push her away, but I'm enjoying the feeling of her tucked under my arm too much.

AMI is waiting for us the moment we come through the door. "Hugo, you are not going to last much longer like this." She gives me the booster quickly and I immediately feel better. I stand up straighter only to see Miya standing in front of me with her hands on her hips.

"What do you mean AMI? Hugo, are you sick or something?"

I hold my arms out. "Miya, you can see I'm not exactly all in one piece here. I could lie to you and tell you that I'm fine, but I owe you more than that. To be honest, I'm glad you're up and doing better. Because my health is declining quickly and my body could fail at any time. You need to know who to contact and where you will be safe before that happens."

"No, absolutely not. There has to be a way to fix you. I mean, take all this shit off if it's killing you."

"It's just a matter of time for me, no matter how I wish it wasn't so. Now no more of this. I need substance and…"Those lines appear in front of my eyes suddenly again. I stand before Miya. Numbers stream through my head as I scan her from head to toe. Her backing away from me startles me out of the trance I seem to be in.

"Hugo? HUGO!"

Her voice seems distant in my head and scared. "Why are you suddenly looking leery of me?"

"Why did your eyes change like that? I was like someone else was looking at me through your eyes."

"What?"

"Your eyes, Hugo, were bright white. Is that normal?"

"It must be a side effect of the booster. I'm sorry if I scared you." She turns quickly and I catch her arm before she bounces off the wall.

"Thanks. So much for running around the planet, huh?"

"Quit pushing yourself. You are already doing more than you should. I didn't think you would be up and walking this soon. It just shows your inner strength."

"I don't feel strong, I feel lost…but Mom used to tease me that I never did things as I should. I never crawled, went straight to walking, and I was talking in full sentences when other kids were jabbering."

I reach over and wipe the single tear off her cheek.

"I'm never going to see them again, am I?"

I shake my head no and I can tell she is trying not to fall apart. "You have every right to grieve, little beauty. You have lost so much and it will take your mind and heart time to adjust. Don't bottle it up, it only makes it worse."

A few more tears fall before I watch her take a couple of deep breaths. Then she smiles sadly at me. "Come on, let's get some food. I don't mind this new trim figure of mine, but I believe I could use a couple of million calories right now. The first time in my adult life that I need another twenty pounds."

I'm not sure what she is talking about, but the mention of substance has me moving. We eat, or I should say I eat, while Miya plays with her substance.

"I have got to figure out how to make us something edible. This crap is terrible. AMI do you guys have an alien cookbook or something?"

"Miya, this has all the proteins and vitamins your body needs," AMI replies.

"Ughh, if you say so, but unfortunately, that's not enough. It tastes like glue."

I can't help but smile at her feistiness and at the moment I realize I can't think of the last time I smiled before she came along. Then she yawns. "You done?" She shoves the bowl away, curling her nose up adorably. I pick them up and put them in the sanitizer before we head toward our quarters.

"Where is your room? Are you anywhere close to me?"

"I'm in the next room. All you have to do is say my name and I'll be there. AMI also monitors the compound constantly."

"Ok, are you feeling any better?"

"I'll make it another rising, little beauty."

She shakes her head. "Why do you call me that?"

"Well, you're tiny, and even though you are different from my kind, there is no denying you are beautiful."

"Wow, quite the charmer, aren't you? I bet you swept all the girls off their feet on your planet."

I walk up to her so close I can feel the warmth of her skin. "Is that what you would like me to do?" I see the hesitation on her face as I lean down, kissing her forehead. I expect her to push me away. Instead, the color of her cheeks change slightly. Interesting.

"Go take your rest, I will see you at rising." I stand in the hallway, watching until she closes the door to her room. As I adjust my shaft, I run a hand across my head. I know I can't want her. She has no future with me, but my body craves her like no other.

The voice of the youngling in the market replays in my head. *'The owner of this toy not only holds your redemption but also your heart. When the time comes, don't let your fears of the last risings destroy your future ones. You are worth something, too.'* Heading into my room those words playing over and over in my head, before I clean up quickly and then practically fall onto the bed, exhausted. The cybernetic below my knee is itching and my back aches where the nerves are inflamed from the infection on my hip from my other leg. "AMI."

"Yes, Hugo."

"Have you been able to find any sort of cure in ENAC's notes for me? The boosters are wearing off quicker and quicker. I can feel my body failing."

"I am still searching, Hugo. You need to rest."

CHAPTER 16

Miya

I hug Poo tight as I toss and turn for hours it seems. The covers are scratchy and I don't know; I feel odd. I get up and throw one of the gowns on that the holo girl had delivered to me. Opening the door slowly, I peek out. When everything remains quiet, I tip-toe into the substance room.

After hitting every button on this replicator, I try several different drinks, hoping there was something decent to drink in the thing, but so far it's proved to be a huge failure. I catch something moving out of the corner of my eye and I just stop myself from screaming out when I see Hugo walk past the doorway. I start to call after him, but something makes me stop.

Instead, I follow behind him as he makes his way through all types of different rooms. He stops a few times and I duck back into the dark so that he doesn't see me following him. I have no idea why I'm sneaking around like this, but something feels wrong.

He pauses, then puts his hand on a scanner of some sort, and a door slides up into the ceiling. He has his back to me and I run in before the door can close. The entire room is nothing but lights and screens. This has to be a gigantic computer of some kind. Finding a darkened corner, I ease my way out of sight, only to have to put my hand over my mouth when I see what is happening. Hugo's fingers start reforming as he sticks them into what looks like ports on the wall.

His head tilts back suddenly as his body jerks, and he screams out in pain. Before I think about it, I jump up. He must have heard me move because his head turns my way, but that's not Hugo looking back at me.

There is a ghostly image all around his face and his eyes are glowing that bright white again. He pulls his hand away from the wall and stalks my way, a sneer on his face.

"AMI!" I scream out as an evil smile stretches across his face.

"What do we have here? You have made this way too easy for me, female. You see, I was in here disabling AMI so I could come to you. But look…now you have fallen into my arms."

I hit the door, trying to get it to open. "Hugo, why are you talking to me like this? Let me out of here! You're scaring me." He grabs me by the back of the neck and slams my face against the metal door hard. Then whispers in my ear.

"Stupid, your entire existence is so stupid. The only thing females are good for is breeding. I have studies that tell me of the euphoria of the act itself. Now, I will finally be able to see and feel it for myself. Don't expect me to be gentle."

Hugo grinds his hardened shaft against me as he pushes me painfully up against the metal door. His other hand rips the gown I have on as he pulls it up. I kick back, only for him to laugh at my feeble attempt to escape.

I can't help screaming when his rough hands start fondling me. "Hugo, please…please don't do this to me! I trusted you."

I feel him stop behind me and his body gets stiff. He releases me enough that I can turn my head. This is when I see his eyes change back to black. He looks down at me and I see the horror of what he has done on his face when he sees part of my gown in his hand. He looks around, but then his eyes start to glow from within again. I whimper.

He smashes his hand against the wall and I fall to my knees hard when the door suddenly opens. Scrambling to my feet, I glance back, only to see him holding his head. His eyes flashed from black to bright white. "RUNNNN!" he screams out and I don't waste a second doing just that.

I can hear him screaming AMI's name as I rush into my room, locking the door. I know it won't stop him for long if he wants in here, but I don't know where else to go. I grab some clothes and run into the bathroom, shoving them on as quickly as I can. I have no idea what to do. It's not like I can call my dad to come get me. With that thought, the tears start flowing.

When the small hologram girl pops up in front of me, I scream at the top of my lungs. She holds her hands out. "It's just me. Come on, we need to get you to a safe place."

"How did you know I was hiding in here?"

"I put a sensor on your wardrobe bot and it detected your distress. You're not alone. SCOUT has Hugo…well, ENAC… cornered. I didn't know until moments ago that SCOUT knew ENAC had hidden somewhere. That male and I are sure going to have a heart-to-heart about his secrets soon.

"AMI has now been reactivated and I believe she is holding Hugo until we can remove ENAC from his processors, but I don't want you to be in harm's way if he gets loose. ENAC will do anything to survive. He has proven that already."

"What will happen to Hugo?"

"I'm not sure, but SCOUT will do all he can to save him. You see that air vent next to the ionizer?"

"Yea."

"Take off the front and crawl inside. There should be enough room for you in there. Make sure you put the front back on once you're inside. Do not come out unless you see me."

She stays with me until she sees that I'm in the air shaft, and then she blinks out of existence. I stay there for what seems like forever until I start to hear voices. I crawl along the tubing slowly since I have no way of knowing if it will hold my weight or not. I take a few wrong turns only to turn back when the voices start to fade away.

Finally, I stop above what looks like AMI's main chamber. I can hear Hugo cussing or I think that's what he is doing because I don't understand the words, but by his tone, you can tell he is not happy.

The holo girl is standing on a stand, off to the side, but the huge male that had been with her when I first woke up is actually manhandling Hugo, trying to get him strapped into a chair. I didn't think holos were solid, but this big guy sure seems to be.

The voice echoing out through the room is creepy as shit. Sounds like something from a horror movie. I can see a couple of AMI's arms laying on the floor in pieces, as others of hers try to help the holo guy with Hugo.

They get him in the chair and straps start securing his body down. They no more than let go of him, that he frees one of his arms and starts ripping the straps back off. It's become a free-for-all in the room. Until the big guy wraps his hands around Hugo's head, the light that leaves his fingers is so bright, it has me closing my eyes.

The room suddenly gets quiet and I can see them re-strapping him down. Dark purple liquid is all over his body and his cybernetic arm is only hanging on by a couple of wires. The shorts he always wears are torn and I can see where his skin is blackened and raw.

Hugo's body suddenly goes limp and I swear I see his life force seep out of his body. "Noooo!" I hit the screen screaming out before I think about it.

"SAGE. Get her out of here!" the big guy yells.

She is in front of me immediately, before she can say anything. "Please, let me go to him!"

"It's not safe for you. The male you know is not who he is right now. He has been infected with a rogue program. The shock SCOUT just gave him, he may not recover from, even if we manage to get the other program out of his main processor."

"I promise I'll stay out of the way, but let me at least stay in the room with him. My voice helped him fight that thing before maybe it will again."

"Why? Why would you take the chance of getting hurt to save someone like Hugo?"

"I don't have that answer, but I can tell you that, until five minutes ago, he was the only one I have felt safe with since I was brought here. And yes, I may have experienced that with any alien I met first. But I feel like as long as he is near, I'm never truly alone. Without the stability of his strong arms, I'm just floating around, lost in a world I know nothing of. I can't explain it, but as different as we are, I have come to care about him, and I think he does me too, in his own growly way, or he wouldn't have been so protective and caring this whole time.

"I'm just as big a stranger to him as he is to me, and my appearance here has done nothing but cause trouble. But not once has he acted like I was a nuisance, or in his way. He has done everything to comfort me. There is more to him than you give him credit for." She stands there looking at me for a minute, then shakes her head yes.

"Ok, I will fight with SCOUT about allowing you in the room, but you have to do exactly as he tells you. You can't get down from here, so you will have to go back to your room and exit the way you came in."

I crawl out as quickly as I can and run down the hallway toward AMI's med chamber. SCOUT points at a place over in the corner and I make myself as invisible as possible. As soon as I'm there, the doors to the room shut, enclosing all of us inside.

SAGE appears only seconds later, standing on a table in front of me. Hugo lays unnaturally still as tears flow down my face. "Is he...dead?"

"No, even though it doesn't look like it from here. He is fighting ENAC. Their minds are caught inside a world we cannot access without killing him. All we can do is wait and watch. If Hugo can push him all at once towards SCOUT, then there is a chance we can trap him."

Suddenly, Hugo arches up and I see the huge holo guy's hand start to turn red, as a ball of light is pulled from Hugo's head. He backs away slowly, the light reaching out everywhere sporadically. But the holo guy keeps it from touching anything. I see him look around, then nods toward SAGE.

She is immediately floating in front of him. The second she appears, the light reaches out toward her. One of AMI's arms pushes me back further into the corner. When the big holo guy and SAGE's eyes turn a bright white at the same time, the light in his hands really starts fighting, trying to escape.

SAGE's eyes flash a bright blue and I swear I hear a scream come out of the light they are holding. I hear SAGE scream, "Now SCOUT!" and the big guy starts compressing his hands together. What looks like little faces appear, all of them screaming, until there is nothing.

The light blinks out, and the only sound now is Hugo's labored breathing. I break free of AMI's arm and rush to his side. His eyes open for a second and when he sees me. He tries to smile, but a cough wracks his already beaten-up frame.

"Little beauty, I can rest now that I have seen your face."

I reach up, caressing his cheek. "Hugo, you can't leave me!"

"Oh, don't shed your precious tears for me, little beauty. You must know that I would never willingly leave you. The moment your gods brought you to me and I held you in my arms, I knew I would be willing to walk into the debts of nothingness just to be granted another one of your precious smiles. Leave this place and go find you a worthy male and let me go. Know that the short time we have had together was worth the pain of waiting for you."

I don't even get to respond. His body relaxes completely and alarms start going off everywhere.

"Miya, dear, step back. I'm going to try to stabilize him until DaR can get here with what we hope can heal him." AMI's arms start working on him all over as I step away from the bed. I hear AMI yell out that she is losing him and then the big hollo guy starts helping detach his cybernetics.

I have my hand against my mouth, trying not to scream. My head feels fuzzy and I can hardly breathe. SAGE floats in front of me. "Miya, your emotions are all over the place. There is nothing you can do here. Let's go back to your room."

I stand here looking at all the screens. I may not be able to read alien, but I'm not stupid. Even I know that when all the lines are solid across the bottom mean. I'm simply empty on the inside. There is no one to turn to. I'm in a place where I don't know how to survive on my own and the only friends I seem to have are computers, or whatever they are.

God, what I wouldn't do to have a hug from my mom right now, or a cup of coffee with Dad as I cried on his shoulder. Mom would tell me to put my big girl pants on, but this isn't losing a job, or my boyfriend cheating on me. Everyone is gone, and I'm now alone. The last thing I remember before the darkness invades my thoughts are strange, unwanted arms grabbing me before I hit the floor.

CHAPTER 17

D aR

"Commander, I just received an urgent message from SCOUT. He needs you to proceed planet side as soon as possible with the experimental prototype if you want to save the male's life. He was able to stabilize his processor and brain waves, but the infection that has spread across his organic body is killing him. Do you want me to proceed with the rest of the plan, or allow the male to pass?"

"No, I would never hear the end of it if we didn't do all we could. If this experiment fails, it won't be because we didn't do our part. And if he survives, then this will give me and him something else to argue about. I enjoy verbally sparring with the grouch. I believe Kira is ready to go, so give the order for them to meet me in the shuttle bay."

I no longer enter the bay when I hear the sound of little feet coming my way. Giggles and laughter follow as they race toward me. Keida launches herself upwards and I catch her in my arms, throwing her high into the air. Her laughter is contagious as I throw her up once again before I put her back down. She immediately starts chasing Danny up the ramp. I shake my head, wishing I had half their energy.

Kira walks through the doorway, and my heart hits my throat. After all this time, she still takes my breath away. Today she has on what she calls a pantsuit and it flows perfectly down her curves. She stops in front of me, one of her knowing smiles gracing her lovely face.

"Whatcha lookin at?"

"You."

"You know, looking at a girl like that, she might think you like her a little bit."

"Maybe a little bit." I reach down, grabbing her by the waist, lifting her up to kiss her gently before sitting her back on the ground because I hear *'ewe yucky kisses'* coming from the two younglings standing on the ramp.

Kira giggles as she turns from me walking up the ramp towards the young ones. Danny grabs one hand while Keida does the other, both of them arguing about who is going to get to sit next to Mamaw.

I was getting ready to have Falcor tell XuL to take another shuttle down when Brittany runs through the door with XuL right on her heels. He grabs her from behind, tucking her under his arm as he runs across the shuttle bay. Their love for one another can't be denied with the sound of their laughter.

"Get your asses on the ship," I say teasingly as XuL heads up the ramp. I shake my head and send out a prayer, simply thanking the Lord of Light for the blessings he has bestowed on me as I walk up the ramp.

The ship takes off effortlessly as Falcor pilots us towards Targres Four. I double-check that the prototype is on board before I head toward everyone else.

Keida meets me at the doorway. "Papaw, are we going to go shopping?"

Danny groans in the background. "Shopping, shopping, that's all girls want to do." I have to act like I'm coughing when she sticks her tongue out at him.

I pick her up and walk over to sit on the couch with Kira. "We might go shopping, but not this rising. We have to take some medicine to a friend who is very sick, and then if I'm being informed correctly, you will get to possibly meet another new friend."

"You mean the new human female on Targres Four who likes the big red guy with metal on him like Unka Tordy."

"How did you know about her, Keida?"

Kira doesn't even give Keida time to answer before asking, "DaR, why didn't you tell us that there was another human found?"

"Keida?"

"Me knows things, Papaw."

"Is this all that you know about her right now?" Her little pink eyes twirl and she shrugs her shoulders before she tucks her head in under my chin. XuL pulls Brittany over onto his lap and everyone is quiet for a minute.

"When were you going to tell us about the girl?" Brit asks me.

"I'm sorry. I should have mentioned her sooner. I haven't known that long myself, and she was in such rough shape, I wasn't sure she was going to make it."

Kira rubs Keida's back, her eyes suddenly sad. "Was she…done like the rest of us?"

"I don't believe so. SAGE will be able to tell you more. She provided her with a few items and is with her right now."

Kira shakes her head. I can see the disapproval on her face. "I thought she had been missing quite a bit these last few days. She is going to get a piece of my mind when she pops back up. I don't like secrets, especially when it involves anything human-related. She knows this."

"I told her to keep quiet until we knew she had survived. From my understanding, she has only been up the last few risings. The last report I was given, I was told she seemed comfortable and was adjusting well. I knew we were going planetside soon and figured it would be a nice surprise."

Keida reaches up and puts her hand over my lips and shakes her head no. "Papaw, be quiet. You're already in trouble. Do you want to get grounded too?" I act like I'm going to bite her fingers before I kiss her on the forehead, smiling as I shake my head no.

Falcor saves me, announcing we would be landing momentarily. "XuL I may need your help getting that box into the compound. I don't remember seeing an inner bay." The shuttle touches down on what appears to be an outer field and the moment the ramp opens; this smell engulfs us.

Kira comes around me as I start down the ramp. "Are these our alien coffee beans?"

"Yes, it is. Unfortunately, this crop may not make it. I'm having some difficulty hiring workers to pick it. Hugo was doing what he could, but I don't believe he even managed to clear one field. I didn't understand how delicate they were to pick until Hugo told me that the machinery destroyed more than it harvested."

"Are you telling me that there could be a possible shortage of my alien coffee?"

"No, my Kira. I will make sure you have enough to make it until the next growing season."

"So, you're saying you will let others go without their alien coffee? This whole universe will be in chaos. "

"Absolutely. You are mine to please, not others. Kira, I know we discussed who Hugo is, but if you feel the slightest bit uncomfortable around him, we will leave."

"DaR, I'm slightly wiser now than I was then. I'm not going to run off. If you no longer have a problem with him, I'll be fine. Now explain to me how these beans are harvested before we go inside."

"I think you simply pick them off the vine. Give me a second, XuL can you run ahead and see if they have a hover stretcher that will fit through the doorway? Ours is too big." Brittany and Kira look around while the young ones play hide and seek through the tall bean stalks. "Ladies, you coming?"

"Oh, yes, sorry, we were just talking. Do you happen to know the girl's name who is staying here?"

"No, let me ask Tordan. He says her name is Miya and as soon as he gets Luna settled, they will also be down. He has not informed her of Hugo's condition, as he doesn't want to upset her further."

We get the prototype loaded and through the narrow hallway. SAGE appears in front of us, leading the way. "Master DaR, please unbox it quickly and then, if you don't mind. AMI will need help to install it into the Crain system we have made while awaiting your arrival. The cadaver will be here shortly."

"SAGE, I hope this plan of yours works, for this male's sake."

"As do I, Master. AMI had to sedate Miya because she was so distraught over Hugo. At least with her being unaware, if this procedure fails, she will be no wiser."

"I have some business at the market, so we will take our leave for the evening. Should we get lodging in the main sector or return here?"

"None of the rooms here are up to your standards, but there are several that are clean and could be converted easily if you would like me to oversee that. I could have Falcor send down another shuttle with the supplies I would need. Actually, that is probably how we should proceed either way, as Miya and Hugo are living in squander.

"I understand that this sector was robbed of its credits, but there were plenty available before that should have been used to make its inhabitants comfortable. ENAC withdrew things like that as a punishment for them being organic and him robotic."

"You have taken care of him, correct? I don't need to guard Kira and the younglings constantly."

"SCOUT destroyed him. AMI is in control of the guard bots at this time, but I can take over those commands and sensors as long as you're planetside."

"I would prefer that. What do you think the male's chances are?"

"This is all unknown. It could be five or ninety-five percent. I have no way of knowing because it depends on the research SCOUT stole from ENAC. He might have been obsessed, but he was of a brilliant design. His calculations and research on this particular subject are astounding. And if this works, this would be a huge medical breakthrough for anyone with a severed limb."

"I'm not sure where they all ran off to, but would you have Kira meet me at the side entrance?"

"She is on her way there now, as are the others. Be warned, she is not happy."

I come around the corner, approaching the side door, when I hear Kira. "She is nothing but skin and bones, and would you look at this place?" I have to hold back my smile when she stomps my way. I love the fire in her eyes when I get that look.

"DaR, have you taken a look at this place? I checked on Miya when SAGE showed me her room, and I swear I have seen animal cages nicer."

"Calm down, love. SAGE is going to work her magic. I had no way of knowing what kind of condition this place was in. I have never been inside and Hugo never asked for anything."

"Of course he wouldn't ask. He was probably scared to ask, or was so used to this…hovel. He didn't know the difference. We are going to the market, right?"

"Yes, my Kira…you can purchase whatever will make you more comfortable here."

"I'm not worried about me. It's Miya."

"Like I said, whatever you feel like you need. The market is in full swing right now and is a short stroll away. All I ask is that you stay with me or XuL at all times and do your best to keep the young ones close." Kira turns away, Brittany and she talking at once, as usual.

I pull Danny over to the side. "Son, this place is dangerous. I expect you to keep Keida close. Because of her odd beauty, she will be noticed, so no running off playing, do you understand?"

"Yes, Papaw DaR, I won't let you down."

I clap the boy on the back, "Never figured you would."

"Papaw DaR, you know how badly the girls get distracted when shopping. I'm going to take my sword with me as I watch over them. Will you and XuL be close?"

"I have something I need to pick up, but I should not be gone long. I will let you know before I go."

The market is busy, but not to the point that I'm worried. Most see me and immediately get out of the way. I walk behind Kira, simply observing the crowd as she makes a few purchases. Everyone is fascinated by her and Brittany, and I have to stop myself from growling when a female reaches out and touches Kira's long hair.

Before we walk to the next stall, I gather her hair in my hand and tie it back out of the way with one of the many hair clips she seems to always have with her. Keida is bouncing all over the place and I smile when I see Danny casually grab her hand so she doesn't wander off.

I see the stall up ahead I need to stop at. "My Kira, I will return shortly." She simply looks up at me and smiles. Brittany asking her a question has her turning away from me. I pull my hood up on my cloak and make my way across the main road, splitting the marketplace.

The vendor sees me coming and motions for me to come inside. He holds up the box, opening it for my approval. I run my fingers across the delicate but precise design.

"You have my thanks. This is astounding and better than I imagined. I have an idea for a few other pieces. Do you have time to discuss them with me?"

He nods and motions for me to follow him. I glance around before I duck through the back door, making sure Kira nor Keida spot me, as I want to keep this a secret.

CHAPTER 18

K ira

The hover container is practically overflowing with all the stuff we have purchased today. I glance around a few more times, making sure that I have made it to each vendor stall, when some colorful fabric catches my eye farther down the lane. XuL has taken the kids to get a snack and Brit is haggling with a pink female over what looks like dog bones for Raven.

"Brit, I'll be one stall down."

"Ok, I won't be another minute. She just has to put these in a bag."

The male running the stall says a few things to me, but my translator isn't picking up his words. I motion to one of the pieces of fabric and he holds it up. Even though it's beautiful, I have no idea what it is. I motion a thank you and just as I start to turn back towards Brit, something catches my eye a little further away from us.

It takes me a minute to comprehend what I'm seeing. DaR is leaning up against a building, his head is down, but his runes are dancing colorfully as a four-armed blue female runs her hands all over his chest and sides. His hood is pulled down over the top of his face, but there is no denying that mischievous smile of his. She takes him by the hand and he follows her inside the building.

I rub my wrist as I'm immediately overwhelmed by his feeling of delight and awe. I have no idea how long I stand here in the middle of the street, my whole world falling apart around me. A single tear flows down my cheek before I wipe it away. I refuse to fall apart here in front of everyone. Turning around, I find Keida standing there, watching me with a frown on her face. I try to smile and act like everything is ok but I know I'm not doing a very good job at it.

Brittany walks and puts her arm around my shoulder. "Kira, you look like you have seen a ghost, are you ok?"

"I just got tired all of a sudden." Keida walks up and takes my hand. She doesn't say a word, but I have a feeling she knows something is terribly wrong.

Brittany pulls me close. "Do you want to head back? I'm ready to go and I think the kids are wearing down too."

"Yeah, that would be best." I'm so devastated I can barely put one foot in front of the other.

"Let me send Danny out and see if he can find DaR. XuL has tried his communicator several times, but he hasn't answered. When he contacted Tordan he said not to worry, that there is something on this planet that messed with their frequency."

"No, Danny needs to stay with us. DaR can take care of himself. We don't want to interrupt him right now, anyway."

Brittany looks at me oddly. "Kira?"

"I don't want to talk about it. Let's get back to the compound."

All I can see over and over is that female's hands on DaR and the same smile he bestows on me all the time. I don't know what to do. This is so not like DaR. Or have I just seen in him what I wanted to? I thought we had a wonderful relationship. We play and laugh together daily. I thought that our sex life was fulfilling and sensual. I mean, I know I'm not the craziest thing in the bedroom, but I never imagined he would cheat on me.

His emotions keep bombarding me. I have to bite my lip to keep from crying out as his pleasure crests suddenly. I can't believe he would do this to me. He knows we are linked together and unless he blocks his emotions, I can feel all that he does. How does he not feel the turmoil going through me?

The next thing that hits my mind is, how long has he been going to places like this? I watch females throw themselves at him all the time, only for him to act disgusted by it. But was all of that an act? I refuse to stay with him now, but where could I go? Even after everything I have gone through, this is the one thing that's unforgivable in my eyes.

I know the girls will support me with the decision to leave, but will this put a strain on their own relationships? I will avoid him until we head back to Falcor, then I will tell him I want to go home. He will send me back to Darverius alone because there is so much to deal with here, and then I'll talk to Tyberius and see if he will help me get my own place. Right now, because of his ties to Earth, he is the only one I know will understand. We make our way back to the compound and SAGE meets us at the entrance.

"Mistress Kira, I am shocked you are back so early. I have prepared Brittany's and your quarters. But there are a few things to finish up before you can retire for the evening. I see you bought the market out."

"Yes, I knew Miya was going to need several more things, and it was quicker for me to purchase them here. Has she awakened yet?"

"No, but she should not be out much longer."

"Mistress Brittany, I have had some toys and entertainment brought down from Falcor for the younglings, if you would like to proceed to that area."

"Sounds great, SAGE, what would we do without you? I think I'll go get out of these sweaty clothes first. And Kira, if you are going to talk to Miya, I would like to come with you."

"I'm not feeling my best. It might be better for you to do it."

"You are still terribly pale. Are you sure you're ok?"

"It must have been the heat. SAGE, if you would lead the way to my room. I would like to lie down. I don't believe I will be attending dinner either. Brit, hug the babies for me and I will see you all in the morning."

It takes everything I have not to fall apart when she hugs me. She has become like a daughter to me and we keep nothing from each other, but I can't talk about this right now. My heart has been crushed and I'm barely holding it all together.

I walk like a zombie down a long hallway. SAGE is talking to me, but I'm not paying attention. I glance around the room, barely noticing the colors or the things she has done to improve the place. I head towards the ionizer and step in clothes and all.

Realizing what I just done, I step back out and yank the clothes I had on off and change into one of my longer gowns. I fall into the bed and simply stare at the wall. I'm sorta blank right now. My mind rolled through question after question. How did I miss the signs? At no point have I ever thought he was unhappy.

I hear the door slide open and I close my eyes, pretending I'm asleep. I have to stop myself from flinching when he sits down cupping my cheek in his hand. "SAGE, is my Kira sick?" I hear him whisper. I can feel his concern. It feels so genuine. It's apparent that he has learned well to project what he thinks I need to feel.

"Let me scan her real quick. With all this going on with Hugo, I have not been monitoring everyone as I should. She is perfectly healthy. I recall Brit asking her earlier if she was ok. And I heard her reply that the heat had gotten to her, and that she didn't feel like herself. I'm sorry, Master, I should have focused more on Kira at the time. I have been distracted."

"I'm sure she is fine, SAGE. Let her sleep. I have some things I need to catch up on, anyways."

He kisses me on the forehead and I have to make myself not move, as I can feel the tears gathering behind my eyelids. I hear the door open and shut and I have to pull the pillow up in front of my face as I fight off the tears. Damn, he needs an award for best actor.

I must have drifted off to sleep at some point because Dar pulling me up against his body as he lies down in the bed has me opening my eyes. I pull away from him, acting like I can't get comfortable. He finally moves away a little bit and I expect him to spoon in behind me, but he doesn't. I can tell he is restless and agitated, as it takes him a while to settle down. I don't move and I keep my emotions locked down until I feel his breathing even out and I know he is asleep.

I lay there listening to him breathe. The warmth of his body, usually such a comfort tonight, is torture. When I finally can't stand it any longer, I slide out of the bed, watching him the whole time, hoping he doesn't wake back up. I grab the first thing I see in my bag, throwing it on quickly before sneaking out of the room.

Even though I make a few wrong turns, I slip out the door and make my way outside. I walk a few feet out into the field of beans surrounding the place and look up at the huge planet in the sky. It's so close you can see explosions and things happening upon its surface with the naked eye.

I run my hand across the branches as I walk along, almost tripping over a sack and an enormous pair of gloves laying on the ground. The gloves are way too big, but because they are worn out, I can still use them. Needing something to do, I start at the end of one row and start picking the small beans off the stalks. I have no idea how long I was out here when I hear Brit and the babies come out. Little Keida runs up, hugging me around my waist.

"Can we play too, Mamaw?"

"Well, I don't see why not."

"Danny, I bet I can pick more than you can," she yells out as she rushes off.

Brittany hip-bumps me. "Have you been out here all morning?"

"Probably longer… Couldn't sleep. But I have managed to clear these last five rows all by myself."

"I might as well help. I'm bored to death. Where can I get a pair of those gloves?"

"I found a few pairs next to that shoot when I was looking for a place to dump this bag. There are extra bags over there, too."

Brit grabs a bag and starts on the other end of the row I am on. The kids are chasing each other and normally this would make me smile, but I have a feeling it is going to take me a little bit to pull myself back together. I feel DaR behind me before I see him.

"What in the frack are you doing out here in this heat? For that matter, what are any of you doing out here right now? XuL, take everyone in until the second sunsets. It gets dangerously hot quickly this time of rising. Now, my Kira, what are you doing out here?"

I refuse to look up at him. "What does it look like, DaR?"

He grabs my arm and starts to yank the bag away from me when I react before I think about it. "Take your damn hands off me. Don't you have someplace you need to be?"

He stands there looking at me like I'm a stranger. I feel my words tear their way through him like I personally cut him, only to be followed by his frustration when I turn back away to reach for the next bean.

"No woman of mine will work in the blazing sun like a commoner."

I step away from him. "Shove it up your ass, DaR. Don't worry, no one can see us here. I wouldn't want to damage your perfect image. You better hope your floozies don't kiss and tell, though, or you're ruined."

He doesn't give me an ounce of warning before he throws me over his shoulder. The beans in my bag spill all over the ground and I can hear the kids laughing as he packs me away.

I am so mad tears are flowing down my face. I have never been good at hiding my emotions and, right now, I'm a wreck. He must have packed me around the building because I can't see the fields or anyone else now. DaR slides me down his front.

I put my head down, brushing the tears off my cheeks angrily, and start to step around him when his hand on my chin, lifting my eyes up to him, stops me. The concern on his face just makes me cry harder.

"My Kira, what has caused this? I hate it when you leak."

I yank my head away from him. "You have no right to act like you care. Just STOP this!" I sling my arms out. "You no longer have to pretend, ok? I saw you yesterday. You made it very clear in front of everyone the company you like to keep. Now, if you would step out of my way, I was busy. Oh, and you can find somewhere else to sleep from now on because you are no longer wanted in my bed."

He looks like I have slapped him. "You will explain yourself right this moment, Kira. I don't like this version of you, nor do I care for your tone."

"You arrogant prick. Quit acting like I'm the one hurting you here. I'm not the one sneaking off from his family to visit a BROTHEL!"

He crosses his arms, his Symbots rolling up and down his arms as he looks down at me with a frown on his face. "Kira, where exactly did you think you saw me, and when?"

I rub a hand over my face suddenly exhausted. "Lord, DaR, I'm not blind, and I'm not stupid. I saw you plainly at the market, leaning up against one of those damn whore houses with a blue, four-armed succubus. She didn't even have to ask you twice, either. You simply followed her right in the door as she stroked you like she knew you intimately. I could even feel how excited you were as she stroked your chest. When you left telling me that you had something to do, you never imagined I'd catch you, did ya?"

"Kira, I will not lie and tell you I didn't go to that brothel, but I did it after I came back here to the compound to check on you. When I couldn't locate you in the market, I became worried. Tordan is the one who told me you all had headed back. I didn't realize my business was going to keep me away for so long."

"What, you went back for seconds? This conversation is over." I try to get around him again, only for him to block my way.

"Oh, you foolish female. I have never seen you act so irrationally. Here…this is why I was excited. I was going to give this to you on the day of your birth, but this is my only proof as to where I was. You can see the receipt inside and the times are on it for this purchase and the other goods I bought later on."

He pulls a square box out of one of the pockets on his pants. He flips open the lid and inside is a delicate comb. His house symbol is outlined in small jewels at the top. "I had this made for you. I know how you love all your hair clips and when I saw this design, I had to have it. This is where I went and why I was delayed because I ordered some for Keida and the other females. You… did not see me at the brothel. I would never do that to you…us. You must have seen, SiN! We have been chasing him all over this planet. And yes, I know he is going to ruin me before we apprehend him. He is always just out of my reach.

"I was told he purchased room and board at that brothel with the credits he stole from this sector. I hadn't told you about any of this because I didn't want to worry you. You mistaking him for me is something I never thought would happen. I went there later with XuL. We were trying to catch him, but he had already been warned of our presence on Targres and was gone. If you don't believe me, you can ask XuL."

Stopping for a second, I push my own feelings to the side and try to replay what I saw in my mind all over again. I was so convinced he was guilty that I pushed our connection away. I can feel his concern, worry, and love pulsing throughout our link now.

He puts his hand under my chin once again, pulling my face up so that I have to look at him. "Listen to me, my Kira. You know in your heart that it was not me. There has never been another since the rising I put you in my arms. You are my heart and soul. It tears me apart that you would even think that I could do that to you, to us."

"DaR, I saw you."

"I swear to the Lord of Light! I will tear that male's limbs off when I capture him! Kira, open your senses! You know my Symbots cannot and will not lie to you. It was not me!"

The fact that his...our Symbots are so agitated tells me the answer. I start to crumble, but DaR's large arms grab me up before I can hit the ground. I tuck my head into his neck as he packs me through the compound, simply enjoying his smell and the comfort that he can only provide me. As I sort through my own emotions, I can't stop the tears when I realize what I almost did to us.

"SAGE, can you have some substance sent to our room? I don't believe my Kira has eaten."

"Right away, Master."

"Go ahead and leak all you need to. As much as I hate it when you're sad, this situation could have become much worse." He lays down in the bed with me still wrapped up in his arms. "I could feel your distance last darkness, but never imagined the cause of it. Promise me this will not happen again. As much as I love your fiery spirit, I seriously dislike it if it's directed toward me."

"I'm so sorry, DaR. When I saw you—him—My heart broke into a million pieces as I stood in the middle of the market. I reacted without thinking."

He kisses my forehead and pulls me so close I felt like we were merging into one. I don't know how long I cried, but once I was done. I felt more like myself.

"Never doubt my love for you, my Kira."

I hear those words over and over as I drift off to sleep. The next morning, I awaken to my gown being magically gone and roaming hands. DaR bites my shoulder gently and I smile as I turn my head to look at him. He rolls me over, throwing a leg across my hips.

"I was recently listening to my boys having a conversation about their females. They both were discussing how much fun makeup sex was. As this was taking place, I felt myself frown at the time, as I didn't believe I had experienced this with you yet. But I believe the last rising occurrence qualifies for such an occasion."

"Oh, you do, huh! Just how much groveling are you going to do to get this makeup sex? I can be quite stubborn, you know."

"I'm well aware of your flaws, my Kira."

"Your odds are going down if you think that is the way to achieve this makeup sex you want."

DaR's roaming hands and all of his little nibbles have me more than worked up. I can feel my own desire coating the inside of my thighs. I'm way too easy when it comes to this man.

He rolls over, pulling me on top of him as he goes. My legs straddle his waist, his shaft seeking out my already slick core. My breast dangle in his face, he looks at them and then smiles before capturing one of my nipples in his mouth. DaR bites and sucks on each of them gently as he pushes me down slowly upon his hardened shaft. My body stretches around his bulk slowly as he kisses his way down my neck. One of his hands grabs my butt cheeks hard as he thrust upward.

I moan out as my body starts tingling all over. I can feel his Symbots expanding from his hands wrapping themselves around me to circle my pleasure button. Their intense vibrations and DaR's thrust has me raising up bracing myself on his chest. My own release rages through me quickly and as I start to scream out. DaR grabs the back of my head, pulling me back down, capturing my lips with his. The kiss is long and sensual; I feel like he is devouring me, showing me with his intensity the extent of his love. He bites my bottom lip, pulling me to him tightly and on the verge of pain as he finds his own release.

I lay upon him, my inner channel twitching from the intensity of our quick coupling. He smacks me on the butt. "Quit moving," he growls out with a big smile on his face.

I can't help but start giggling as he tries to hold me still because he, too, is overly sensitive right now. I squeeze my inner walls around him again, only for him to pick me up off the bed with his shaft still fully seated inside of me. Each step he takes pushes him in and out of me, relighting my need and want for more. We no sooner make it into the bathroom and close the door when I hear the door open and little feet run into the room.

"Mamaw, Papaw, where is you? Mommy said we were gonna play a game outside now that it's cooler. You wanna come, or are you still feeling yucky?"

DaR pushes me against the wall, slowly easing himself in and out of me. I smack his arm playfully as he holds me here with a big smile on his face as he continues to tease me. I try my best to sound normal. "We will be right out, honey. You go on."

"Papaw, you better not be kissing in there."

"Why? I like Mamaw kisses."

"Yuck, adults do the grossest stuff. I'll be outside."

We hear the door close and we both start laughing. "You heard her coming, didn't you?"

"Yes, it was a good thing she wasn't a few moments earlier, or we could have scarred the youngling for life. We are going to have to start remembering to lock our door."

"As much as I'm enjoying all this, you know she will just come right back if we don't show up soon." He grinds himself into me once more before he walks both of us into the ionizer together. DaR had just sat me on the counter of the sink in the bathroom and was gradually making his way back down my body with very little resistance from me when I hear the door open again.

"Mamaw! Are you really that dirty?"

"I'm on my way out."

I hold my hand over my mouth, trying not to laugh at the frustrated look on DaR's face. I point down. "You may need to wait until that goes down before you head out." I kiss him on the chest as that's the easiest place for me to reach. I start to open the door only to stop and look back at him, watching me in the mirror.

"I love you, my big gray alien."

"Love you, my little human."

CHAPTER 19

M iya

I wake up hugging Poo tightly only to find myself in strange but familiar surroundings with no idea how I got back to this room. I fling what looks like fresh blankets off me and throw my legs over the side. I have to hold on to the headboard to get my feet under me, as I stagger to the bathroom before I pee on myself. I sit on this weirdly shaped commode, trying to figure out what happened last. My mind seems slow and unfocused as I finish up. When I go to wash my hands, I look up at the mirror.

Have you ever stood in front of a mirror shocked to see yourself looking back at you? I don't feel like I'm really here. I'm simply standing off to the side, watching someone else live their life, my life. Any moment now, I expect to wake up and this will have been nothing more than a weird dream. The girl looking back at me is a stranger, someone lost within themselves. My eyes look too big and my full lips dominate my face in this new slim version of me.

Taking some water out of the sink, I run my fingers through my hair, trying to calm these unruly curls down. I head back into what I reckon is my new bedroom and spot my bag on the shelf above the bed. I pull it down, open it up slowly going through the things I thought I couldn't live without one at a time.

Tears flow down my face when I look at the scattered things laying on the bed beside me. I throw the cell phone and so many other worthless things back in the bag. Until I come to a picture of my parents and me. I rub my fingers down their faces tracing their familiarness. Opening the jewelry box I sob when the little ballerina no longer twirls around. Closing it back, I hug it to my chest, crying out as I struggle with this new reality.

"Hello,… Miya." The sound of someone calling out my name has me jumping. The very sound of another human's voice has me looking up, I wipe the tears from my eyes as someone walks through the door. Suddenly, standing in front of me is one of the most stunningly odd-looking girls I have ever laid eyes on. Her curvy frame is set off by long dark hair and practically black brown eyes, but it isn't her human features that catch my attention. It is all the dark markings all over her skin. At first, you think the markings are tattoos until they begin to move on their own.

"You're up. I was starting to worry. How are you feeling?"

"Are you human?"

"Mostly, yeah, got a few extra things going on here though." She motions up and down her body.

"Your tattoos are moving."

"They kinda do that. I have gotten so used to them I no longer notice. If you think this is weird, wait until you meet my other half. I'm Brittany, by the way."

"Lord, I'm sorry… looks like I left all my manners on earth. I was thinking just before you came in that I might possibly be having an out-of-body experience."

"I believe we all have had that thought at one time or another here. All of us have had those freak-out moments. The good part is that I can guarantee you that you have awakened in the safest of odd realities. XuL and I have traveled a lot and let me assure you after seeing what I have. I'm grateful every day that he was the one who found me."

"How long have you been here?"

"A while. My trip was not a pleasant one, but that's a story for another day. I have come to love this new world. In time you will too. Right now, that goal seems far away, but each day will make it easier. Life deals out its cards when it's ready. I could have never dreamed up my mate or even my little girl, but here we are. Luckily I'm surrounded by people I have come to love and so that helps on the days you miss the ones that were left behind."

"We can't go home, can we?"

"No. I don't know how much you have been told, or even how much you already know."

"It's not much. I can remember Mom, or maybe it was Dad, saying something about a storm. They called it a planet killer. I begged them to let me stay. I remember fighting the straps and mom reaching out for me. Dad grabbed her, pulling her away, just as the pod closed around me. The next thing I know I'm here — Ohh my god, Hugo. Is he ok?"

I start to run past her, but she grabs my arm stopping me. "SAGE has the med chamber sealed. They won't let anyone in, but as far as I know, he is still alive. Sit down, I'll try to answer any questions you might have. Then we will talk to SAGE and see if it's safe for you to at least visit him for a minute.

"Kira normally handles all of this hard stuff, but she wasn't feeling well. So, I volunteered. The storm your parents were telling you about tore the planet, our planet, apart. My mate's brother RaZ and a few others barely made it off the planet before it exploded. None survived as far as we know."

I sit here looking at her, the words she said simply refusing to sink in. Everything and everyone I have ever known or loved is gone. How do you work through that? How do you rationalize that without any kind of closure? Then I remember, "Wait a minute, you mean no one survived? There were ships all around me ready to be launched."

"You were the first one found in one of those. Once you were recovered, DaR sent EvO out to search the outer regions of the galaxy to see if he can find any others. You were only days from death when they finally got your pod opened. The odds of anyone else surviving much longer is slim."

I look away from her as I fight the tears. "What a damn nightmare…I'm never going to see my parents again. I'm never going to…I can't do this right now. If I start dwelling on it, I'll drown in my own tears. You know what is crazy? I feel like I went to sleep and got right back up."

Brittany was rubbing my back gently. "We all woke up disoriented, half-starved, and confused."

"I'm weak as a kitten, and even when I was younger, I was never this skinny."

She rubs her hands together and smiles beautifully over at me. "The good thing is, chunking you back up won't take long and your days of being hungry are over. Now, you adjusting to all of this… that has affected all of us differently. I think seeing all the different types of Others was and is still the hardest for me. My own mate is beautifully scary to look at. His harshness is only surface-deep, though, so don't go running off screaming when you do see him. XuL calls me his Kismet and swears that I'm the only female in the universe for him. I would have never believed those words if they had come out of a human, but these males have a way of convincing you. These markings show our bond. Our daughter also has them."

Running a hand through my hair, pulling at the knots, I shake my head. "Hugo tends to growl all the time and half of what he says

I have to cipher or guess at. When I think about it, it was his kindness that kept me from being terrified in the beginning. As sad as this sounds now, I couldn't see him though. My eyes were messed up. So, I got used to his voice before being shocked at his appearance. And, wow, you even have a daughter. I don't even know what to say to that. I have so many questions, but they are all running together."

Brittany pats my leg. "I promise, things will get easier. We have to be close to the same age. Were you still in school?"

"I was a sophomore in college."

"I had just graduated high school when I got my free trip across the cosmos. What were you studying?"

"I was majoring in chemistry. I wanted to go to perfumery school. I have always loved perfumes and makeup."

"No way, that's impressive. Alana will have to hook you up with CIP. He is the most unique program ever. He specializes in makeup and clothing. I bet you two could work together and produce some marvelous scents."

I feel a moment of excitement. "You mean I might be able to do that…here?"

"I don't see why not. A girl has to have a passion in life; all of us like different things. It makes for the craziest conversations when we all get together."

"How many?"

Brittany looks like she doesn't want to answer me. "You are number seven."

"Only seven. There are only seven survivors. Like seriously, seven!"

"Maybe eight. I forgot about Danny; lord don't let him hear that."

"Do you all live here?"

"Oh, no, we are simply visiting. DaR had some work to do here planetside and then there was the evil scientist ENAC that captured Tordan. That's another long story. We seem to have all kinds of those. I know all of this sounds like a bad C-rated horror movie we would watch back home, but it has been insane here for months.

"Anyway, Tordan saved Luna and now they are totally into each other, so all this craziness has worked out. Since there have been a few security breaches too. The guys decided it was best if we all come along. You know, the speech *you're safer with me than anywhere else.*' We actually live on Darverius. I honestly don't know how long we will remain here. Keida is missing SeeSee, so I don't believe we will be here much longer. She tends to get what she wants, as you will soon learn. You will love Darverius' not earth by any means, but it's beautiful in its own way."

I look away from her. Why is the thought of leaving here bothering me?

She touches my arm lightly. "You won't be forced to go, of course. Don't sweat the little stuff right now. There will be plenty of time to make those sort of decisions later. Do you want me to see if you can see Hugo?"

"Please."

"SAGE, you listening?"

When the little holo girl pops up out of nowhere, I barely stop myself from screaming.

Brittany laughs at my reaction. "You will get used to that, too."

"Mistress Miya. I apologize for neglecting you. My programming is being pushed to its limits with being so far from my main dwelling. Do you approve of the improvements I tried to achieve in this small room of yours?"

"I do, and thank you for making it look less like a gray box. Do you think there might be a way I can see Hugo?"

I watch SAGE look over at Brittany. "He is not in his best condition right now. It may be disturbing for you to see him like this."

"I don't care. He never left my side when I needed him most, and I would love to repay that. I will stay out of the way; you won't even know I'm in the room."

"Give me a moment to discuss this with AMI. Miya, In the meantime, you should grab something to eat. Mistress Brittany, General XuL has come up with a game that Mistress Kira is calling it a bean party. I'm sure you'll want to participate. With that being said, Mistress Keida is looking for you for this game to commence."

"SAGE, tell her we will be in the cafeteria. Come on, Miya, let me show you how to use the replicator, especially if you want some actual food. The guys can't even cook with a machine doing it. I swear XuL just hits a button and hopes for the best."

CHAPTER 20

Miya

Brittany hits a few buttons on the food thing and out pops what I swear looks like a cheeseburger. She hesitates to give it to me. "Don't look so excited. It's not a cheeseburger, but it's as close to one as you will ever eat again. I promise it's not bad, though."

The sound of someone running catches both of our attention. A little girl rushing past me and up to Brittany has me stepping back out of the way. "Mommy, I have been looking everywhere for you. Was you hiding from me?"

"Looks like you found me. I wasn't hiding. I was talking to Miya."

When she turns towards me, I gasp. She is pale green; her features are so delicate she looks like a porcelain doll. Bright pink eyes stare knowingly back at me, like a child with an old soul. Long brown, pink, and silver hair hangs messily clear past her butt. A few dark symbols on her arms and neck match Brittany's.

"Miya, this little ball of energy is my daughter, Keida."

"You are stunning."

"Thank ya, it pays to be cute, especially with so many Unka's. It helps get ya stuff. Do you want to come play too? We are going to have a bean party. Daddy said that for every bag me and Dan filled up, he would give us a credit I can spend tomorrow at the market. I mean, I could get anything and not have to ask. This is so awesome. So, hurry up and eat. I got credits to gather."

"Why don't you go on out? I'll be there shortly."

"Opay, Miya, we will play later," she yells back as she runs out of the room.

"Yeah, you don't have to say it. I know she is slightly larger than life. And a whirlwind on top of all that personality."

I can't help but laugh at the look on Brittany's face. "I can tell you have your hands full with her, but wow, she is going to be a heartbreaker."

"Yea, I tease her that she would have been easier to raise if she would have been ugly. But there isn't a male alive that will ever be good enough between her dad and the rest of the males in her life."

"That's normal for most kids, isn't it?"

"Most kids don't have twenty-two Unka's, as she calls them, to warn off every suitor she will ever have."

"Twenty-two! Someone needed to be sat down and explained clearly how to prevent that."

"Ohh, that's hilarious. I can't wait to tell DaR that one, anyway that's another long story."

SAGE pops up on the table. "Mistress Miya, if you are done, I finally managed to get you clearance into the med chamber. I only have to walk you through a sterilizer before you can enter. We can't allow any outside germs right now. His body is too vulnerable."

I throw the rest of my not cheeseburger down and stand up.

Brittany, grabbing me for a hug, startles me, and I have to bite my lip when I feel tears building up. "Go ahead, spend some time with your growly male. I apparently have a bean party to attend. If you need anything, don't hesitate to have SAGE contact me."

I follow SAGE as she floats in the air in front of me. "Close your eyes once we enter through those doors. You will feel a cool mist cover you from head to toe."

I step through the doors and immediately close my eyes, waiting for her to tell me to reopen them.

"You're good, but I need you to understand this before we go into the room. The only thing you can touch is his organic hand.

Don't touch any of the wires or even try to wipe any blood off of him. Do you understand?"

"Yes, keep my hands to myself."

"And, Mistress Miya, his appearance will be shocking. Here shortly we are going to try to attempt a procedure that has not been used before. That's how I got AMI to agree to let you in. He may not make it. Do you understand what I'm telling you?"

I wipe a random tear off my cheek. "This may be all the time we have together."

The door opens in front of me and I have to press my hand against my mouth to keep from crying out. SAGE warned me it would be shocking, but that was not the appropriate word. There is nothing left of him. I knew parts of him were metal, but I didn't understand the complexity of how much.

He is a torso, with one arm and half a leg. He is laying there in pieces. Open wounds where his cybernetics were attached have what looks like plastic wrap over them to keep his nerves and things from falling out. I walk slowly around the operating table he is on and sit down in the chair next to his bed.

I can't seem to stop the tears now that I have seen him like this. Hugo raising his hand up to wipe the tears off my cheeks startles me. "You're awake! How are you awake? Lord, Hugo, you're a hot mess."

"It's not all bad. You did just say I was hot."

I can't help but giggle at his attempt at humor. "Are you...can you feel anything right now?"

"I'm missing a few parts, but to be honest, the pain has lessened considerably since SCOUT and AMI removed the cybernetics. I'm glad you came. I wasn't sure if you would. I'm not exactly pretty right now."

"You are the most handsome red alien I know."

He growls at me, "I'm the only red alien, you know."

"Either way, it's the same. I have been trying to get in here to see you since I woke up." I reach up and grab his hand in both of mine, rubbing along his long fingers and claws. He coughs and all the monitors in the room start beeping. A couple of arms start moving around him, checking vitals, and bandages. I don't know what to say. I stare down at his hand in mine and how our colors are so different, but the same.

"What is the cause of that frown, my little beauty?"

"I...don't want to lose you. It sounds stupid when I say it out loud. I mean, I have only known you for a few days. And where I'm from, falling for someone this soon is unheard of. Some would say I am simply lusting after you, but I need you in here." I pull his hand over my heart. "I have lost everything that was ever dear to me, and if I lose you, they might as well put me in the same box because my heart can't handle losing anything else. The moment I opened my eyes only to realize I couldn't see, I latched onto your voice. You became my safe haven. You took care of me like I was yours to cherish. I told myself that you cared for me like you would no other, that I was special. My heart grabbed onto that attention like a sponge, absorbing your every touch and kindness."

He cups my cheek. "You were and are mine to cherish, my little beauty. Know that when you can feel nothing else. I may not survive, and your life will continue on without me. But know that I will search for you in another life, as I await you on the other side of this one. Cry no more,… because we will not be separated long. Or if you feel the need to…cry, do it because you miss me, not because you won't see me again."

I lean my head down and kiss the top of his hand. "I will be right here; you fight for us."

I get a smile only a second before SCOUT appears behind his bed and injects him with something that makes his whole body relax.

"Mistress Miya, we are going to start with the procedure. I have no problem with you attending as long as you sit right there. This procedure may be disturbing and quite bloody. If that bothers you, please go ahead and step out of the room."

"I'm fine. I don't have a weak stomach." He nods his head and the next thing I know, there is another body being lowered into the room. It's another of Hugo's kind, with an enormous hole in the middle of his chest.

SCOUT nor AMI say a word, as multiple hands work on the dead guy. SCOUT pushes a round cylinder to the foot of Hugo's bed and over what was left of his leg. I see red lasers pulsing and numbers flashing all over the room. I grip Hugo's hand tighter when I suddenly see a saw appear in one of AMI's arms. SCOUT makes an odd noise that almost sounds like a fax machine before his eyes start glowing an eerie white. A clear divider lowers between me and the other bed right before AMI starts dissecting parts off the dead guy.

SCOUT has to be reading my mind unless I asked him out loud what they were doing. "Mistress, this procedure has not been tested and is completely experimental. I was able to review the prior AI's research and, with the help of AMI and SAGE, we took his work to the next level. We used some of the technology we already had and merged them together, creating this portable device.

"Unfortunately, we are fighting against time as Hugo has extensive and prolonged damage. When we ran his essence, we immediately calculated that he could only be repaired with one of his own race. SAGE immediately applied for a newly acquired cadaver as we needed fresh tissue to transplant. However, the cadaver had to be of the same size also and at least partially from the same gene pool. So many things had to match. Hugo's chances were becoming lower and lower with each of our calculations.

"We were not sure Hugo would make it long enough to find the unfortunate candidate. Fortunately, one was reported once we compared the samples given to us, we reimbursed the family and took the body in the name of science. I had to cut farther into Hugo's body in order for this to even have a chance of succeeding. AMI is calculating the exact measurements and we are going to try to attempt this smaller transplant first. The machine should be able to bond every nerve and blood vessel as it attaches the muscle and skin.

"We will know quickly if there is any reason to continue on with the other procedures. Because the piece being connected will discolor quickly once it's removed from its host. They will not do so if it's reconnected properly."

"So, you are saying you might be able to give him his legs back?"

"The end goal is to reattach all of his appendages. But at this point, his chances are slim because of his already deteriorating state. If this would have been a fresh injury in the field or a battle and the part removed was still available, according to our calculations, we feel this machine could regrow the severed part and reattach it with full success. This could save many a soldier, no matter the species.

"This will also become a standard part of all Medical facilities if successful. Not only could it save lives, but it would give many their quality of life back. The sad part is the AI who did most of this research was withholding it for his own gain. So many lives were wasted over his selfishness. The appendage is ready, and we will proceed now with the first attachment. Are you sure you want to remain in the room?"

"I'm not going anywhere."

He nods, then one of the arms passes the lower part of the dead guy's leg and foot to SCOUT. He positions it inside of the machine, once again making that odd computer sound, his eyes flashing from blue to bright white. All I can figure out is he is talking to something. He readjusts the leg a few more times and then the machine looks like it shrinks down on the inside.

The machine makes all kinds of crazy sounds and SCOUT never takes his eyes off it. It releases way quicker than I would have thought. There is no way that was long enough to reattach something. He moves the machine off that leg and onto the other one. Maneuvering the machine in place again and then starts the procedure all over. AMI hands him practically an entire leg this time and I see the machine clamp down once again.

From where I'm sitting, I can't really see the one he just connected, even when I try to stand up a little bit. The machine blinks and he moves it again, only this time it seems like every arm AMI has emerges out of the ceiling and I have to duck when I feel one brush over my head.

They start attaching what looks like thousands of wires and needles to the parts that were just connected. Hugo looks like a pincushion. I watch little lights pulse up and down the wires.

I turn my head when I hear SCOUT cuss. He keeps adjusting the arm, but the machine won't grab onto it. Picking the top of Hugo's body up, he practically pulls him off the bed. Something comes out of the floor to brace Hugo's upper body as SCOUT attempts to get the shoulder lined up. This time the machine flattens out before it wraps all the way around his side, holding his shoulder in place.

I swear you could see the relief on SCOUT's face when the machine started making the fax machine noises again. "This is why I was designed to shoot things out of the skies," I hear him say.

"I take it this is not your day job?"

"Correct." He holds his armored arms out. "As you can see, I'm not built for this type of work, but at this time, besides AMI, I was the only one programmed to operate this machine. I have its design encrypted until we see how this procedure goes. The form you see in front of you is also new to me, and becoming solid was not something I anticipated, but has proven beneficial."

"You definitely don't look like a doctor. You look like a soldier."

"This is my preferred form, as protection is my chief operative."

The machine beeps once again and SCOUT drags it away. Once he has the cylinder out of the way, he picks Hugo up and repositions him back onto the bed. I grab his hand immediately. And even duck out of the way a few more times as AMI's arms work quickly to hook up all these lines. The parts they put on Hugo are lighter red. "Do you think it was successful?" I am almost scared to ask.

AMI's voice makes me jerk. "SCOUT, so far the limbs are showing stimulation from the incisions all the way through. If this continues and his body doesn't reject them, then his chances are rising slowly."

SCOUT simply disappears, and I shake my head. I'm never going to get used to some of this crap. "AMI, was the other body younger? Is that why they're a different color?"

It takes AMI a moment to answer me. "Forgive me, Miya, I was so focused on aligning the electrodes I didn't hear your question at first. Hugo's skin has been severely damaged from working in the fields. Master ENAC didn't care that the second sun's rays were destroying the organics, he simply wanted the job done. I have treated Hugo many times in the past for sun sores. I have full intentions of reversing the skin damage now that he will be unconscious for a few risings at least. This will lighten his skin, making everything match somewhat better. You should rest while you can. He isn't going anywhere. I have him highly sedated. We can't take the chance of him awakening too soon or moving around."

"I'm fine. If I get tired, I'll go over and crawl into the big chair in the corner. I don't want him to wake up like this for the first time by himself."

"You are good for him. I have become quite attached to him as the past rotations occurred. He suffered much at the hands of ENAC, took beatings for other organics, and helped me here with many operations when needed. I kept his and Luna's communications with each other quiet so that Hugo wouldn't feel so alone. His species live in family groups, and being alone slowly destroys their will to live. SCOUT destroyed his memory block when he pulled ENAC's evil presence from his processor. I fear he will be greatly bothered by his past."

"When he awakens fully, will he still have that processor thingy?"

"He will, but it won't interfere with anything we have done now. I'm going to update the transmitter so he can communicate with me or the other AI with a simple direction of thought. Luna and Tordan both will still be able to communicate with him, as well, because of their implants. Later, if you would like the same thing installed, we can look into it."

"Nope, I'm good. Stay out of my head. If I can't hear your voice, I don't need it. This Luna, they were close?"

"Not in the sense I think you might mean. Luna's memory block completely wiped her mind. She thought she had been born here and the pieces of metal she had been installed with were from her faulty genetics. Of course, all of that was false, but she was easily manipulated and controlled. Tordan took her from here because she was also deteriorating and injured badly. Falcor has ways of mending one such as you. I received a communication from Falcor earlier confirming that Luna was fully healed and adjusting well. Hugo was her only friend and Tordan has asked us not to mention any of this to her unless we felt like he would survive.

"Luna is like you, in a sense. You both have lost your home world and, because of how it happened, it seems like it was just last rising. Even though she had been here for several Orbital rotations, the moment her memories resurfaced, it was like she lost them all over again. She will have a hard time combining her past and present."

I lay my head down on the side of Hugo's bed. "I'm trying not to think about it. One day it will all hit me and I'm going to fall apart. Right now, I have Hugo to focus on, and I know that's helping. My mind is in complete denial that everything is simply gone. I mean the hows and whys simply flow through my mind constantly, and when he is healed, I will seek the answers, but until then, I need to keep putting one foot in front of the other."

Hugo's legs twitching catches my attention. "Is that normal?"

"At this point, I don't know the answer, Miya. However, I figure any movement from top to bottom is a good thing. SCOUT should return shortly. He is double-checking some sensors in the outer fields and as extraordinary as this sounds, he has been working on another machine to help with the bean crop while assembling this one."

"He seems a man of many trades. "

"He is third in command of Falcor, the largest building and cybernetic infrastructure on Solaris, and in charge of some of the primary defenses on Darverius. He is still doing all of those jobs while being present here. He is an extraordinary male indeed."

The side door opens, and a tray floats forward, SAGE directly behind it. "I'm happy to hear you approve of SCOUT's many talents because, AMI, he is already spoken for."

I turn my head away to hide the smile on my lips. SAGE is the size of SCOUT's forearm, but she is all personality.

CHAPTER 21

Miya

The days pass slowly as I watch him heal. I sleep occasionally, but no matter how many times they try to get me to leave, I refuse to. Thankfully, there is a bathroom and what they call an ionizing shower attached to this room, or I would stink by now.

There have been a few close calls with Hugo and the attachment of his arm, but for the most part, his body doesn't seem to be rejecting his new parts. I have walked all around his body, marveled at the changes taking place.

I have sung lullabies and told him about my life and my dreams as I held his hand through the nights. His body twitches randomly and SCOUT still startles me when he pops in and out. I hate this waiting game.

Brittany has brought me a few books, and I even read them out loud, hoping that the sound of my voice at least lets him know that he is not alone. AMI started removing some of the wires from one leg earlier, and little lines of dark purple blood ran down the bottom of his leg where it was attached below the knee.

"Miya, I require your assistance."

"Yes, lord, anything. I'm about to start doing jumping jacks or even running in place over here."

"This should provide you with some stimulation. The leg I just removed the electrodes from needs to be massaged and exercised. Do you think you can lift his leg by yourself? His muscle mass is quite solid now."

"I will do my best." One of her many arms hands me a cloth to clean the blood off and what looks like a thick lotion. I clean him up as well as I can and then start working my way down from his knee.

"Miya, you will need to do his entire leg."

"Oh, my bad. I was just working on this new part."

I start all over again, moving the towel that was draped over his hips before I think about it. Laying on top of his inner thigh innocently is his…junk, worm, private parts, bringer of intense pleasure. What do you call…ahhh, that? I toss the covering back over him quickly, shocked, and now fantasizing. The sight of that thing is now burned permanently in my brain forever. Soft, he is larger than the few males I have seen back home. I mean, there was no missing it, just lying there. It was slightly darker than the rest of his body, with black raised swirls going all around it.

I make myself focus as I start again at the crease of his hip and work my way down, cleaning the dried blood off as I go. When I start applying the thick lotion, I wonder how much fun I could have with this stuff if he had been awake. I'm a total perv, as every time I work my way back up his leg, all I can think of is what that lovely red thing would look like when he is aroused.

The machine they did this with is a miracle worker. If I didn't already know about his extra parts, his body isn't going to give up its secrets. Because I have to look really close in order to see the seam where the two pieces of flesh were merged together. I giggle as I work the lotion through his huge toes. The man's feet have to be like a size twenty or something. I stop suddenly when I realize these are not actually Hugo's feet. "AMI, were Hugo's feet this big?"

"My calculations are very accurate, but because of his genetics, they could have been larger."

He seemed big before and all that metal was a little intimidating, but now that he has been…remodeled, he seems alarmingly huge. I didn't pay much attention to the cadaver they brought in, except there was no missing the massive horns the other guy had. I can't imagine how painful it was for Hugo when his were removed, or for that matter how much bigger and threatening he would appear with them.

"Miya, when you finish with that leg, could you apply the same lotion to his chest around his electrodes? I produced this lotion to help with rejuvenating his damaged skin."

"Why is his skin getting darker in places you guys didn't operate on?"

"The damage the sun did to his skin kept it red. His body was constantly trying to repair the damage. As it completely heals, you will start seeing other colors dominate the torso. He had an intricate marking on his chest when he arrived here, but ENAC cut it out so he would have no proof of his origins. That place will probably darken more than any of the others."

"I'm sure glad you guys destroyed him because I swear I would have found a way to unplug that bastard. I'll be careful not to get too close to the wires." I have no idea why this feels more sensual than his leg did, but damn, it does. The feeling of his muscles running down his chest and stomach under my fingers is like tracing a rare piece of art I have coveted from afar. I rub the lotion around the side of his neck, practically laying over his good side. I stop when I notice his black depths staring back at me. Moving back slowly, his eyes trace my every move. "AMI, I think he is waking up."

"How could one slumber with your hands all over them little beauty?" he whispers.

I grab his face in my hands. "Hugo…don't move a muscle. You are almost completely healed and you should not be awake yet. I can feel your body tensing up under me. Just take a couple of breaths. I promise everything is ok."

"It can't be too bad; you are here with me." He starts to turn his head and I pull his face back to me gently. "Hugo, look at me, nowhere else. Just focus on me right now. You know I have missed you. It's terribly quiet around here without all your growling. Are you hurting anywhere?"

His eyes roam all over my face, settling upon my lips. "I know what would make me feel better, but if I'm not allowed to move you are going to have to help me with it."

"Are you thirsty?"

"Oh, I am, but not for what you think." Before I realize he is moving, I feel his large hand grasp the back of my neck, settling firmly in my hair as he brings my lips to his, crashing his mouth into mine. His lips move firmly against mine until I yield to him. A moan leaves my lips, and he uses that to part my lips as his tongue delves deep into my mouth. My entire body suddenly aches with need. I have been kissed before but nothing like this. I can feel my nipples getting hard, and dampness starting between my legs as I lean fully against him.

Realizing what I'm doing, I push away from him gently. Rubbing my fingers across his lips. "If you want more of that, you have to stay still." I see one of AMI's arms come up behind the bed and inject something into one of his larger ports.

His eyes start to go in and out of focus. I keep my hand on his cheek until I see he is resting once again. I plop down in the chair next to his bed and run my fingers through my hair. "Damn, that was intense."

AMI's voice has me looking up. "He should not have awakened that soon. I had to double his dosage. It truly must have been your touch that awakened him. It's strange because he didn't react to my hands on him at all. There must be something in your skin that calls to him. But we still need to apply this lotion to him a few times a day. Maybe I should ask if one of the other females will come in and apply it."

"Absolutely not! I will wear gloves the next time if need be, but he is mine to care for. Not one of the others."

"I had a notion you would say that. We will figure it out."

He sleeps for another two days. AMI and I start moving him around more after she removes the last of the electrodes. Both of his legs appear to work properly, but his shoulder seems really stiff. I have a feeling it will give him some trouble, but at least his skin isn't rotting off anymore.

SCOUT comes once again to double-check on his progress and gives the ok for AMI to start reducing his drugs. "AMI, I'm going to clean up real quick and maybe take a quick power nap while you are adjusting his meds. I'm so tired I can barely function."

"He should still be out for at least half a rotation. Once he awakens, he will have to learn how to walk again, and this may take some time. I'm setting up an area to rebuild his muscle memory on the other side of the room as we speak."

I strip my clothes off and run into the vapor shower thing, throwing on the next outfit in the pile SAGE provided me with while I have been in here. I'm excited for him to wake up and scared at the same time. They didn't discuss or tell him what their plans were before they fixed him back up. I wonder how bad it will bother him when he realizes he is wearing another man's arm and legs.

I come back into the room only to see AMI marking the inside of Hugo's arm with a symbol of some sort.

"AMI, what are you doing?"

"What I hope does not prove to be a mistake. I warned them this should be discussed with Hugo before it was applied, but Commander DaR is not used to being told no. Hugo has always been a proud male and I don't know how he will react to being marked by another."

"What does it do? Mark him as property or a bad person?"

"No, it's a sign of high standing actually, and it's not given freely. Honestly, I was shocked when Falcor gave me the order directly from Tordan to have you both marked. This is a House symbol. The House of DaR, to be exact. Very few are granted this sign of family and safety, especially from DaR. This will make things much easier for Hugo in the outside world and provide the best protection for you as well."

"So, I'm supposed to get it too?"

"All the human females are marked. Do you remember Hugo telling you about Mistress Kira not being marked and the horror that followed?"

"I do."

"If you think that Commander DaR becomes deadly when it comes to his female. I would warn you that Hugo would become uncontrollable. He has lost too much in his existence now,… and if you were taken, he would tear the universe apart until you were found. This mark is a warning of the house that stands behind you. The males of the House of DaR are the most respectable and deadly in our known solar system."

"Ok, you talked me into it. Where do I sign up?"

CHAPTER 22

H ugo

The sound of multiple voices all around me startles me awake and I open my eyes, only to see Tordan's ugly face close to mine.

"Well, hello sleeping beauty, glad you could join us."

"Frack you, you ugly bastard." He pats me on the shoulder and turns to talk to someone behind him.

AMI's eye swivels down in front of me. "How are you feeling?"

"Like it's too loud in here! Where is Miya?"

A gentle touch has me slowly turning my head. My heart practically stops beating in my chest when I see her smiling beside me with tears in her eyes. "Hello, little beauty." A sudden voice in my head has me looking around the room.

"See,… I was right. You are a big softy."

"Luna?"

A small female walks around Tordan I don't recognize at first. "What? Don't I get a *glad to see you* or nothing, or are you saving all that sweetness for Miya?"

"Luna? Praise be the Lord of Light…look at you. You're beautiful."

Tordan pulls her back against him. "Hey, no flirting with my female. I'm right here. Don't think I won't take advantage of you being in that bed to kick your ass, because I will."

When Luna suddenly smiles, I swear I become speechless. "Luna, I never imagined all that was hiding behind what they did to you. Are you well? Do I need to kick Tordan's ass?"

"I'm perfect, but thanks for backing me up. I haven't been up and about long myself, but I had to come when they said they were waking you up. At first, I struggled with coming back here, but SAGE has made the place look like a whole other building. Tordan and I will be here for a few days, and we have a few things to talk about, but you're popular today, so I'll see ya later."

She reaches down and kisses me on the cheek, and I'm over-whelmed by her new look. I reach for her, only to stop and look twice. I sit up suddenly. "What the frack!" I have two arms. I hold what used to be my cybernetic arm out, twisting it back and forth. The muscles in my chest feel tight and my arm is stiff, but…I can move my fingers.

"AMI, what is this sorcery? How did you make my cybernetic arm look like this?"

I rub the area on my shoulder with my original hand and the skin is no longer blackened or sore to the touch. I run my hand down the other one and I swear it feels real.

AMI's eye darts in front of me again. I know there are others in the room, but it's like I'm hearing them from a distance. "Hugo, take a deep breath. Right now, I need you to ignore everyone else. I want you to stick both of your arms out straight and move your fingers."

Slowly, I move them out where I can see them.

"Do they feel somewhat the same? Is one heavier than the other? I need you to think about it."

"Both seem fatigued like I have been working all day, but that's probably from lying around."

"I'm going to give you this ball, and I want you to squeeze it as tightly as you can."

The ball bursts apart from my grip when I take it in my original arm. I hear DaR laughing in the background. "Tell him to turn those down a little, AMI."

She hands me another one, and I put it in what I think is now a covered cybernetic arm and I crush it, but not like I did with mine.

"Excellent, we will have to work on that arm some, but it's responding better than I anticipated. That's all we're going to do while everyone is here. Give yourself a moment to relax and enjoy your friends."

I marvel at my new arm. Amazed at the fact it doesn't hurt at all. As I am rotating my wrist, a mark on the underside of my wrist has me stopping. The entire room gets quiet as I rub my hand across the house sign.

DaR had moved up to the side of my bed while I was distracted looking at this mark. His house mark… Angry, the words come out before I think about it. "What is this, a mark of ownership for me? Did I go from one master to another? Am I your property now?" I snarl out. I'm so angry I barely notice Miya putting a hand on my chest, trying to comfort me.

DaR smirks down at me. "No, you stubborn bastard, it's called family. You can thank me later. Oh, and while we are on the subject, the fields are finished, and the note paid. There were enough credits left over to provide anything else you may need once you are back on your feet."

"How? Why…? Why would you do this to me?"

He turns around, pointing at all the people on the other side of the room. "Once again, it's called family. That's what a family does when one of their members needs help. They pull together to get it done. With that being said, we have lots to discuss when you're better. This sector needs you and I can't wait for SCOUT to expand the new machines. Enjoy this downtime while you can. We are going to head out for the rest of the rising. I have some young ones who want to spend their credits at the market."

I will never admit it, but when he grabbed my arm in a warrior's pledge, I had to fight the tears in my eyes. Settling back in the bed, I fight the emotions that seem to be bombarding me. I can hear Miya talking to a few other females, but it's all jumbled up.

I can remember the rising I tried to take DaR's woman, like it just happened. I can still recall the feeling of his blade sinking into the arm I was holding onto her with. Then I see them, the males who were with me at the market. It's sad, but I don't remember their names. We served many battles together, but that's all I can recollect. My memories… they're coming back slowly.

Miya's sweet voice pulls me out of the past. "Hey, you ok?"

"I'm not sure. What do you think of this new covering on my cybernetic arm?"

She glances around the room like she is waiting on someone or something. "Well, it seems like they have left the explaining up to me. So don't shoot the messenger and don't give me that look either. I know you're confused, but no growling at me. Ok, here goes nothing. Move your toes."

"Miya, I don't technically have toes."

"Just try."

The moment I do, I yank the covers off that were covering my lower body. I try once again and my toes move. I have toes... where did they come from?

"Miya, how?"

"I can't talk to you while Mr. Peppermint is staring up at me, so cover him up until we can get you some shorts or something." She points at my cock as I look at her.

I hesitantly drape the sheet back over my hips, but refuse to cover up the rest. I keep moving my toes.

"Ok, here's the deal, and like I said before, don't shoot the messenger. Because I'm not really qualified to answer the questions I know you're going to ask, but I'll try. SCOUT, SAGE, and AMI took ENAC's research and, from my understanding, built a portable machine that could reattach flesh. Especially flesh that had been severed, or torn off. Are you following me so far?"

I nod, still not understanding anything she is telling me.

"Then...well...crap, they brought a dead guy in who was the same size as you. You know, because your own parts were not simply lying around here somewhere...they had to find someone else's... I'm so screwing this up! Anyway, they cut off his legs and his arm and used that machine to attach them to your body. It took days to get the nerves to restimulate, but your body accepted the transplant, and you look great."

I move the one leg up that I had lost beneath my knee, looking at where I know the cybernetic was before. I run my original hand down it. The skin feels real when I pinch it lightly. Miya is standing in front of me, wringing her hands together. I look up at her, trying not to snarl. " You watched them cut another of my kind up and put his parts on me?"

Miya shakes her head. "Yep, it was educational. Glad I never wanted to go into the nursing field."

AMI swings back into the room. "Hugo, are you ready to see if you can stand?"

"Where the hell were you when he was asking about all this?" Miya yells out.

"Miya, I was listening. You did quite well, and his vitals never changed."

"AMI, you put another Phogx male's parts on me?"

"Hugo, that is apparent. There is nothing wrong with your vision. You could only be repaired with another of your kind."

"Was he killed… Did you take his life to save mine?" He suddenly sounded so distraught.

"No, Hugo, he was terminated, unfortunately, in a training session. SAGE had asked for all cadavers to be reported with measurement and family essence. The match came in only rotations before we believed we were going to lose you."

"Why didn't you simply make me new cybernetics? "

"Your body was too frail, and organics were never meant to be merged with metal."

"The family was compensated and even told what the body was being used for. They considered it an honor and a way for their son to live on, by using his limbs to save you. If you regain full functionality, the machine will be implemented everywhere. It will save thousands of soldiers that are injured on the field. Because the design comes from this facility and your body was used. Commander DaR has made sure the majority of the profits remain here to be used as you see fit."

It takes me a moment, but I'm able to swing my legs over the side of the bed.

"Hold on a second. You can't get up and just let him flop all over the place. AMI, do you have any shorts in here that will fit him?"

One of AMI's many arms emerges out of the ceiling, holding a pair of my old shorts. She lays them next to me and I try to straighten them out.

"Here, give them to me." Miya leans down, and one at a time, slides them past my new feet and up my legs as far as she can.

"Hugo, try to lower yourself down slowly until your feet touch the ground. See if you can feel anything as you put your weight on them."

I slide down the side just a few inches, the coolness of the floor almost overwhelming me as I have not felt that in so long it takes my mind a moment to recognize it. I smile when I realize I'm able to stand up. My legs are wobbly but holding my weight. Miya shimmies the shorts up. Just as her face gets to my crotch, the sheet falls off and my cock bumps right against her cheek. She stops dead in her tracks.

I grab my cock immediately, moving it out of the way, embarrassed as I expect her to be furious. Instead, she looks up at me, laughing. "Your junk just bounced off my cheek, didn't it?"

"My junk?" She nods her head towards my cock.

Before I can reply, I start to sway back and forth. She pulls my shorts the rest of the way up, then grabs me around the waist.

"Steady there, big guy. The last thing we need is you falling. You know I would never be able to get you off of the floor on my own, and I know you would rather stay down there than have me get one of the others to come in and help you."

"You ought not see me weak like this either. I should always appear strong in your eyes."

"Are you fucking kidding me right now? I have literally watched you fight for your life these last couple of weeks. Now, look at you standing here. You are the toughest guy I know, so quit with the alpha male shit. Now, do you want to sit back down, or do you want to try to take a few steps?"

"It doesn't bother you what I am now? Pieces of a dead male."

"Lord, where do you guys come up with this crap? Listen to me. I don't give a shit if they had made your legs out of wood, metal, flesh, or even left the damn things off. I'm not standing here holding you because of your looks, or parts, as you put it. I'm here for the male who bathed me when I was so disgusting, he had to hold his breath. I'm here for the male who never left my side and let me cry when I needed to. I'm here for the kindness you seem to only show me and a select few others. I'm here for you dammit, so quit trying to push me away. Don't piss me off because, right now, I could probably kick your ass."

For the first time since I opened my eyes, I'm glad I have two arms because I use them both to pull her close to me. "You are an extremely convincing female."

"That's better. Keep the compliments coming. Now let's do this. Prove to the entire universe that you are more than a few spare parts."

I manage about three steps before I have to stop. A few of AMI's arms come out of the ceiling and they insert themselves under my arms, trying to relieve some of the weight off my new legs. I manage to walk from one side of the bed to the other before I'm shaking all over. Miya helps me roll into the bed and I flop back like I have been working in the fields nonstop.

"You did great. I can't believe how well you're adapting. You've got to be hungry; rest for a little bit, and I'll run out and get us something to eat."

Shaking my head yes. I try to hold back the tears until she is out of the room. I pull my legs up to my chest, feeling the bones and skin underneath my new fingers. The tears flow down my cheeks as it finally hits me. What a blessing I have been bestowed. I'm whole again. I have a home of my own, a job, and the possibility of Miya.

For a few minutes, I let the tears flow before I wipe them away. I will not let my new family down, nor her. I will use this second… third chance I have been given to be worthy of the house mark I was granted, and hopefully Miya's love.

However, I have to get back on my feet. I can't take care of her if I'm bedridden. The more I think about it, the more I realize I must talk to Tordan. I will need his strength to get me farther than this bed. "Tordan?"

"It's good to hear your voice, Hugo. What's on your mind?"

"I wasn't sure if I was still able to communicate with you this way. As much as I hate having anyone in my head, I'm glad to have the security of knowing you're a simple thought away. If you have some extra time next rising, I need your assistance."

"We will be here for a few rotations. Luna isn't going to leave until she makes sure you're ok. With that being said, what can I do for you?"

"I need you to teach me how to walk."

"I'll be there at first rising."

When Miya comes back in, I'm more focused. The smile she bestows on me as she puts the tray on my lap is worth any discomfort or extra parts I will have to endure.

CHAPTER 23

H**ugo**

Miya brings me the oddest food, but it sure was a vast improvement from the mash I was used to eating. "Thank you. That was delightful for a change."

"You're welcome. I hope to be able to cook you an actual meal one of these days. You probably don't have a local Walmart or grocery store around the corner, though, so our meals will be a lot of trial and error. Too bad we don't have pizza on speed dial for when I mess up."

"Am I supposed to know anything you're saying?"

"Nah, I'm just rambling."

"It's been a worrisome couple of weeks, and having you to talk to is nice. You stayed with me here the whole time?"

"Yep, we are getting plenty of use out of that big chair in the corner. It's become a favorite piece of furniture for me."

"I have not been the only one recently in need of a healer. How do you feel, little beauty?"

"It's… I'm having my moments of weakness, but I'll be ok. My mom always told me to never look back, to always look forward. We leave the past behind us for a reason."

"I too have started to recall some of my parental units' words, and have come to believe that sometimes forgetting is easier than remembering. I disgraced my family with my foolish actions and, up until this rising, I had forgotten."

"AMI said your blocker had been removed. Now that you can remember your family, are you thinking about contacting them?"

"Never, not only would they refuse to acknowledge my existence, but now I could be tried and charged for my crimes against DaR. That male died that rising on Darverius, and Hugo was born."

"So, Hugo is not your given name?"

"No, but it was close. Ugolan Myr Phog was my birth name."

"I like Hugo better. My mom named me after a character in one of her favorite horror books. Miya Ann Sawyer."

A bottle of lotion suddenly lowers down from the ceiling. I take it out of AMI's hand. "Oh, I should have already done this."

"What is it?"

"It's lotion. I need to rub it all over your skin so your old and new skin heals properly. That second sun left some nasty marks on you."

I look down at my chest, noticing some peeling and darker spots. The dark red inflammation that made my skin hurt if touched seemed gone, mostly.

Miya drips some of the thick liquid on the bottom of my legs, and I immediately want to pull away. It feels like a thick lubricant and the smell is offensive. She starts humming while she rubs it into the muscle of my calf. When she starts on my feet, I can't stop the reaction of jerking away.

She starts laughing as I move my foot from one side to another to keep her from applying any more of that nastiness. "Are you ticklish?"

"No, but I don't like it!"

"Hugo, it's just lotion. It's good for your skin."

She reaches for my foot again, and I tuck it under my other leg.

"Oh, quit being a big baby, and give me your foot."

"I don't like it! What is your word…it's yucky."

"Ok, I'll give your feet a break, but we have to at least put this on your chest and back."

"The frack we do. Tell AMI to knock me back out. That stuff is disgusting."

She puts it up to her nose. "Does it smell bad or something?"

"Yes, and it feels like snot being rubbed into my skin."

She starts laughing so hard tears are flowing down her cheeks. "Here you are, this big bad hunter, killer, and total alpha male extraordinary flipping out over some lotion. If your enemies only knew all they needed to make you surrender was this little bottle."

"Female, this is not funny. That substance is horrid. I will crawl out of this bed if I have to."

"Well, what is the old saying? If you're not willing to listen, you better be willing to feel! And here I was just thinking about how much you would enjoy feeling my hands all over you."

"You don't need to use that nastiness as an excuse to touch me."

"No, but it was a good one, and you need this. Your skin needs it. Let me put this on you now and then I'll see if I can find something less miserable to apply from here on out. If I had my chemistry set and the right herbs, I could make something myself."

"I will allow it one more time, but don't think that even your pretty words will get me to do this ever again. And what do you mean you would make me some?"

"I was going to be a perfumer, well before my whole world took a trip to an alternate universe."

"What is this perfumer? And why can't you pursue that here?"

"You know it's the smell good stuff all girls like. To be honest, most guys do too, but it takes stuff. And I'm not sure where to start with alien flowers or herbs. Back home there were books and different plants we could experiment with, here I wouldn't know where to start."

"We have purchased scents available in some select places. Our market does not have these because there are no local vendors. However, if this is something you would like to pursue, I see no reason why you cannot. We have books and learning holos too on most subjects. I am positive what you need could be obtained."

"It's nice to know everything I ever wanted to do is not lost just because I'm here. Maybe one day we can look into it, but right at this minute, you are here to suffer at my mercy."

"Be quick about it, female. I'm not sure I can remain still for long." Miya doesn't hesitate to start on my chest. The smile on her face keeps getting bigger every time she looks up at my snarl.

However, the longer her hands are on me, the less the lotion bothers me as her gentle touch makes me shiver all over as she caresses every muscle on my upper body. My cock starts hardening the lower she rubs on my stomach.

Suddenly, I see the sheet starting to rise even with my shorts on. Embarrassed by my body's reaction, I try to think of something else. Unfortunately, the more I watch the expressions on her face, or when she bites that little tongue of hers, my cock refuses to behave and I feel like a young male who is about to embarrass himself. Considering it's been Orbital rotations since I even considered laying with a female, I will probably react like a youngling again, ready to explode with the touch of her hand.

I grit my teeth and press my lips together to keep from moaning out when she leans across me. The feeling of her breast pressed up against my side has me gripping the bed to keep from dragging her up here with me. Her innocent brushes against my cock have me biting the inside of my jaw. Miya, giggling, has me grabbing her wrist.

"Enough of this torture! My control only goes so far, Miya, and you have pushed me to my limits."

"Oh, you are tougher than that. I was just getting to the good part."

"Have mercy on me, little beauty, or I'm not going to be responsible for my actions."

Her hand eases lower beneath the sheet and I grab her wrist before she can go any further. "Miya, you're not blind. You can see how my body is responding to your touch."

She bites her lip before smiling mischievously. "I'm just doing my job here. I can't help it; we are both enjoying all this a little too much now. Just lay back and relax. I still have parts of you to rub down, now quit being difficult."

"Miya, the only thing you have not touched is aching for you terribly right now."

"We can't leave anything out, so let's get these shorts off of you. Help me raise your hips up so I can finish my job properly."

I have no willpower when it comes to her and the very thought that she might touch me there has me helping her remove these shorts as quickly as possible. She is seeing this new body of mine completely bare and, for once, I'm glad I still retained some of my original equipment. I grab the base of my cock, stroking it hard, trying to relieve some of the pressure only for her to knock my hand away.

"Hands off, mister. You are supposed to be relaxing."

She starts rubbing that thick crap all over my hips and all around everywhere I want her to touch, teasing me relentlessly. I even move my hips towards her so that my cock is brushing up against her arm, but she simply moves away. At this point, the second she does touch me, I'm going to explode. A drop of my own essence runs down the sides of my cock and I see her stop for a second, watching it.

She stops long enough to take a piece of cloth, wiping her hands off, turning back to me. Without an ounce of warning, her little tongue licks across the top of my cock and I practically scream as my whole body lifts upwards.

"Looks like we have one more part that may need my attention." She grabs my cock at the base, both of her small hands wrapping around it, stroking it slowly. I grab onto her hands with mine, applying more pressure. My hips moved up and down with her every stroke. I grunt as the pleasure is almost painful. I can't remember the last time someone else besides myself has touched me like this.

Once again, she gives me no clue as to what she is going to do next. Miya leans over me, looking up at me with a wicked smile on her face before she takes me in her mouth. I have to make myself not grab onto her head as she explores me. When she pops me out of her mouth suddenly. I take a breath I didn't realize I was holding. She is merciless when she licks me from top to bottom, only to then suck me down as far as she can.

Never in all of my fantasies did I ever imagine a female such as Miya would ever pleasure me so. I fight my release, not wanting this fantasy to end. Until her small hands start to caress my balls as she pumps me in her hand up and down. "Miya, I'm going...to cum." I try to move her away, but she just sucks me harder. My release hits me so fast and powerful that I practically black out. The moan that leaves my throat I know the whole compound heard. She continues to nip and lick at me until I'm boneless laying here.

Miya pulls my shorts up, grinning the whole time. "Now, isn't that better? As your nurse, I believe you need to rest now. That last round of meds seems to do the job."

"You wicked, wonderful little creature."

"Yeah, yeah,… you loved every minute of it."

I can't stop yawning as I'm talking to her. "You have no idea, little beauty. Have you heard the phrase, paybacks are hell?"

"I look forward to it, but today it's all about you. Now that you are all relaxed, you need to get some rest. Your body is still healing."

"I don't want to sleep by myself and I don't want you in that chair either. Come up here and lay down with me. I will behave."

Miya looks at me and then at the bed. "What if I roll over on you or kick you in my sleep?"

"How about we compromise? Crawl up here and lay on my good side. If it's uncomfortable, you can get up after I fall asleep."

She scrambles up next to me and I pull her close, tucking her into my side. I hear her sigh and her body relaxes as one of her small hands rests on my chest. She must have been more tired than she let on because it wasn't long before I felt her breathing even out and her body slacken.

I lower my head down so my face is pressed into her curls. Inhaling the scent that is all Miya, smiling when her leg moves on top of mine, I thank the Lord of Light for the sacrifice of that other male and the gift he gave me of being able to feel her through our skin. Then her parents for their sacrifice as they forced her into that pod.

Closing my eyes, I feel more content than I can ever recall. I don't believe I ever slept that well in all of my years.

CHAPTER 24

Hugo

An odd sound has me opening my eyes. AMI has darkened the room, so I know it's still dark outside. The sound happens again, and I look down at Miya. Her mouth is slightly open and I smile when I realize the noise is coming from her.

The happiness this little female provides me with zero effort on her part makes me realize how much I care for her. How did I make it a single rotation without hearing her voice or seeing her smile I'll never know, and I hope to never find out again.

It hits me then that she may not stay here when DaR and the others leave. But the very thought of Miya depending on anyone else guts me. She fills the empty space inside me I didn't know I had with her mere presence, even though she is different from me. To me, that's what makes her so sexy.

I could sit in a chair and simply watch her forever, but I want more than that. I am a greedy male and I want her to be mine. How do I convince her to stay with me? I won't demand that she stay, but now that I hold her in my arms, I know I will want her until the Lord of Light takes my last breath, whether she is here or not.

When she kissed me for the first time, I felt as if I was the luckiest male alive. What do other males do to keep their females? I understand that treating them well and providing food and shelter is a must. These things I can provide her with now, but there has to be more.

I look down upon her sleeping face. As I kiss the top of her head, I comprehend the emptiness that plagued me before. Can I survive without this now? I refuse to find out. I will do all I can to prove to her my worthiness, but I must get my strength back in order to do that.

Unwrapping myself from her arm and leg slowly. I slide off the side of the bed, my feet tingling on the bottoms. I try to take a step, but my muscles are not responding automatically.

"Hugo, have you awakened?"

"I have Tordan, and as humiliating as this is, I could use your assistance to relieve myself."

I look over towards Miya, still in the bed, and pull the sheet up over her more securely before Tordan walks into the room. I motion for him to remain quiet as he approaches. Tordan nods his head and clutches onto my waist, lending me his strength as I take each step.

My whole body moves oddly the more steps I take. He gets me into the refreshing chamber and once I have a hold of the stand, he steps back out to give me some privacy. Looking up at the mirror, I barely recognize the male gazing back at me. I pull my braid back out of the way and scratch my horn bases, which have become sore.

I haven't taken ten steps, and I can already feel my legs shaking. I can hear Tordan talking to Miya; even though we tried to stay quiet we still managed to wake her up. I step back out of the room, wobbling and grateful for Tordan's strength.

"I want to thank you, Tordan, for your assistance."

"You would do it for me."

Those words hit me hard because I have never been that male. I always focused on myself and what I wanted first. If someone else benefited at the same time, then that was fine. Would I do this for him? I hope the male I am fighting to become doesn't have to think about it. I look over to the bed, only to notice that Miya is gone.

"She went to get cleaned up and changed and then she was going to grab some food. I told her to go ahead and eat with the other females. That we would come shortly."

"Looks like I owe you once again for getting her out of the room."

"I didn't figure you wanted her to watch you struggle. Your pride would never stand to look weak in front of her."

"I have already accomplished that more than I'm comfortable with. I feel like a youngling trying to take his first steps right now."

"Well, technically, you are. Good thing you're a determined bastard, huh? So it looks like AMI has an entire area set up for you to stretch these muscles out. Let's get to work."

By the time we got done, I felt like I had run around the planet. "That's it. I have nothing left."

"Come on, just one more time."

"Frack you, Tordan, you pushy bastard. I'm going to fall on my face."

"Ok, youngling, I will give you a quick break. Luna wants a minute with you, anyway."

"Youngling my ass, I have more rotations on me than you do."

"Not with these new enhancements you don't."

He helps me over to Miya's chair, and I practically fall into it. At least I can stand and walk across the room on my own now, but my battle legs are going to take a while to build back.

Luna walks in and I swear I can't stop staring at her. The eyes I know well, but other than that, she is a familiar stranger. Tordan kisses her on the forehead. "I'll give you guys a few minutes. I need to go speak to DaR."

She pulls a smaller chair over in front of mine, then takes my hand in hers. I rub her small hand with my fingers, amazed at its delicateness. She smiles sadly up at me. "That one is still cybernetic. Can you believe it? SAGE and all the others, well, they know their stuff."

I just sit there looking at her. "It's strange to actually hear your voice, instead of it just being in my head. Luna, you are glowing. I never imagined ever seeing you like this. When Tordan took you from here, you were barely holding onto life. I was afraid it was the last time I would ever see you. Have your memories returned?"

Luna shrugs. "They have and there are days…well, I'm sure you understand better than some. Tordan is great. They all have been, but you were my friend when I had nothing else. When Tordan told me what they were doing to you and the fact that you knew nothing about it, you can say I got slightly upset, but in the end, I'm happy they went ahead with it. Because look at you now."

"Is Tordan treating you well? I can't kick his ass at this moment, but that won't always be the case."

"He is wonderful and really more than I deserve. We, that's me and you Hugo, we finally have a family. It's odd because it was just you and me against the world before. I know I never said anything, but there were many a night that if I hadn't had you to talk to, I would have given up."

"Luna, you have been the only thing I even slightly cared about before, but my feelings for Miya are different from what I felt for you. I'm not sure what love is, but I'm willing to do anything to figure it out. I can't live without her. How do I keep her? The feelings I have for Miya are new to me, and I'm terrified. I'm not enough for her. What makes a male worthy in your kind's eyes?"

Luna smiles, and her beauty takes my breath away. "Probably not what you would think. The first thing you need to learn is that males and females don't think alike. Most of the time, they don't even want the same things. But I can tell you stability, a pleasant home, love…those are the most important things. However, I believe as long as she is with you, she could care less where you were at.

"I've had time to talk to her and, even though she is young, she has a good head on her shoulders. She is determined and isn't letting her grief pull her down or dictate her future. I would say just be yourself, but we know what a grumpy ass you can be. So try to smile, and even though you want to be everything she needs, don't forget to be true to yourself first."

"What if I can't?"

"Can't never could do nothing, and that's not the male I know you to be. This weakness you are fighting will pass. You have your whole life in front of you. Learn to enjoy it and smile more. You are quite handsome when you do."

Tordan comes walking back into the room. "Hey, I heard that. I know Hugo is not better looking than I am."

Luna rolls her eyes and I laugh. "He's fishing for compliments again."

Tordan picks her up and sets her on his lap. "Ok, while you have us here, use us for all its worth. You need something better for your girl than that square box you call a bedroom. Some of the best decorators and designers are sitting idle in the gathering room. How are you planning on using their skills?"

"I can't ask nor take advantage of them until I do something first. Would you help me down the hallway, Tordan?"

"I'm not carrying you bridal style, if that's what you're asking, but I can hook an arm around your neck and drag you." Luna elbows him in the side and I see him act like it hurts.

"Come on, let's get your big ass up. You're lucky she is here, or I would just throw you over my shoulder."

Tordan kisses Luna gently before he sets her on her feet and off to the side, out of the way.

Luna blows me a kiss before saying, "I'll go on ahead. You guys take your time."

I sit, admiring the love in his eyes as he watches her walk away. "Doesn't it scare you that she will pass into the beyond before you do? What do you know of their life spans?"

"I have been blessed with a true mating. In order to heal Luna, I gave her some of my blood and the nanites created a life link. A blessing I never imagined even possible. Unfortunately, not all humans will be linked to their mates. I didn't know if you knew that SAGE has perfected a healing chamber that can heal their bodies. The machine they used on you was similar in design. Because of this medical miracle, we believe as long as they are regularly treated, unless it's an unfortunate accident, there is a possibility of them living past us."

"Best news I have heard this rising. My Miya is young, but I know how quickly youth leaves us all. I have lost track of my own seasons, but I know I have rotations on her."

"That is one thing our females care nothing about. Thank the Lord of Light or we would all be a bunch of old, heartbroken males."

CHAPTER 25

H ugo

For some reason, the substance room never felt this far away before. I hear laughter and the sound of multiple voices as we get closer. Tordan gets me to the doorway and steps back, letting me go in first.

I don't make it two steps before I hear the sound of a sword being pulled and a small male human jumps in front of me, blocking me from coming in any further.

"Who are you? How did you get into this compound?"

Miya jumps up from the table where she was sitting with the others and I motion for her to stay.

"I'm Hugo. Who may you be, young warrior?"

The male stands barely to my waist and I hear Tordan cough behind me, trying not to laugh. I start to step towards him when his eyes start to glow an eerie blue, and his hands take on a ghostly outline. You could feel the male's power throughout the entire room.

A dainty youngling female comes up behind him and gently touches the arm he is holding his sword with. "Danny, this is Hugo. He is the reason we came here. This is Luna and Tordan's friend. This is his dwelling."

The male pushes her behind him, never taking his eyes off me. "Is this accurate?"

"The female tells you the truth, even though I have never seen one such as her."

"Such as what?" the boy practically growls back at me.

"One of such delicate, but intriguing features."

He lowers his sword, never taking his other hand off the younger female as he backs both of them out of the way. He doesn't take his eyes off me, but I do see him relax some when Tordan walks around me, ruffling the boy's hair as he walks past him.

I look at the boy, impressed with the fact that, even though I am triple his size, he was going to protect his family. "May I enter?"

"It's your home. I apologize if I have offended you."

"Never apologize for protecting your own. You will make a fine warrior one day. May I have your name?"

"My name is Danny."

"And you little female?"

"Oh, I'm Keida. That's my mommy over there, and Daddy is out helping Papaw DaR."

I look over toward the other females, immediately noticing Kira. The woman I almost took from DaR and the reason I lost my prior life.

Turning towards her, I see her stiffen up as I get closer. I know my appearance has upset her, and that's the exact opposite of what I wanted to achieve here. A few steps away from her, I lower myself down slowly onto one knee and bow my head.

"Mistress, I know that I wronged you in my prior life and I ask for your forgiveness."

At this point, the only sound in the room is the beating of my own heart as I keep my head bowed, awaiting her answer. The feeling of cool, soft fingers touching my arm has me looking up. She has tears in her eyes and I can see her lip quivering slightly.

"This is not something I expected out of you…Hugo. I knew you were the main reason we were coming to this planet, but I will admit, seeing you walk through that door terrified me. We have all done things in our past that we wish we could do over. My rash decision cost you your life that day. Because of that, I believe I should be the one apologizing."

"No, Mistress, my behavior that rising was unacceptable. The only regret I have is the unintentional terror I put you through. My upbringing raised a better male than that and I hope that one rising you will see me as a friend." Struggling, it takes me several tries to arise from the floor. Gratefully a strong hand grabs my arm, pulling me the rest of the way up. I stand at full height only to come face to face with DaR.

He looks me up and down for a moment. I don't know if he is considering my sincerity or going to kick my ass. Someone tapping me on the hip has me glancing down. The youngling female is looking up at me with bright pink swirling eyes when she raises her arms up. I look back at DaR, not understanding what she wants.

"She wants you to pick her up."

I reach down, grabbing her by the waist, holding her out away from me. The smile she grants me lightens my heart as I bring her closer. She pulls my braid around my shoulder, playing with the end of it before she looks at me. Her eyes twirl like pink liquid, the color quite shocking against her pale green skin. I have no idea what she is looking for, but I swear I can feel her presence inside my mind. Before I came in here I was worried and stressed about the things that needed to be done and my own weaknesses.

Suddenly, I feel like a great weight is lifted off my shoulders and a peacefulness I never imagined engulfs me. It takes me a moment to realize this youngling is the one calming my thoughts and feelings. "Thank you, sweetness, for the gift you have bestowed me."

I kiss her on the forehead and sit her back down, only to watch her head towards the human boy before they run out into the hallway.

DaR's dark voice startles me out of my deep thoughts. "She has a way of knowing what we all need. I wish I had the same insight as to what we could do to give her the same peace.

"Hugo, I wanted to let you know we will be leaving next rising. Some of the perimeter sensors are going off randomly at our main dwelling on Darverius, and I feel the need to check them personally. There is no reason for us to remain here any longer with the fields in and the fact that we have ran out of leads on the whereabouts of SiN. We need to return to Darverius as I have pressing matters to attend to at home."

He looks away from me and to his mate. "My Kira...ladies... start packing your things. SAGE informed me this rising that Ickis has returned from his yearly mating season with several more little ones. I fear we are going to be overrun before long if he doesn't quit dragging them all back home.

"RaZ also contacted me moments ago, updating me that both him and Katherine have started walking the main perimeter with Raven and the other hounds. The Selin Queen is in her nest and she seems overly anxious. Telling them of a strange presence in the dark forest. She is keeping the other Selin close to her. RaZ says she keeps showing him one of the Guardians, but he has not been able to locate it yet."

"Commander DaR, I have no words for all that you have done for me. Not only personally, but with the compound, too. I'm eternally grateful for your assistance, and all you have to do is ask, and I'll be there. Before you leave, I do have one more thing to ask of you."

He crosses his arms and smirks at me. "I want you to take Miya with you. I have no dwelling or anything to offer her as of yet. I don't want her living in this squalor." He puts his head down and I can see he is trying not to laugh at me and I can feel my own anger building.

He reaches out, grabbing my shoulder. "You have a lot to learn about our human females. I believe you are about to get your first lesson." He moves out of the way and I see Miya standing there with her hands on her hips.

"Miya?"

"Don't *Miya* me! I'm a grown-ass adult and I decide where I want to go or stay. Do we understand each other?"

"It's not that I don't want you here! You have to know that, but you should not be living in a place such as this."

"What? I have food and a roof over my head, and you. I'm not saying that later on when you are back to your full strength, that I don't want to go see these other places, but I'm not leaving you. Where you go, I go. So, if you want better for me, then make it happen. Whatever we decide, we do it together because as far as I'm concerned, you are the rest of my life."

I don't remember taking the steps, but I have her in my arms before she finishes that last part. She wraps her legs around my waist and I kiss her like my very life depends on it. Laughter behind us brings me back to my surroundings. I lower Miya back to the floor, pulling her in close to my side.

Tordan has his arm around Luna's shoulder, both of them smiling at me like they are up to something. Luna claps her hands together, practically bouncing. "Oh, this just makes the surprise so much better now. Tordan, my love, would you help Hugo up the steps?"

I look down at Miya, and she shrugs. We walk out into the hallway and then up toward the upper warehouse. Everyone comes out of the substance room, following behind me slowly as I make my way up the stairs.

The door to the warehouse is open and I stop dead the moment we enter the large space. Everyone fans out in front of me, nothing but smiles on their faces.

"Kira, would you like to take the floor?" I hear DaR say.

"Hugo, Miya, while you were in recovery, us girls were talking about the living arrangements here in the compound. At first, we were going to have the men knock down a few walls hoping to make you a nicer living area below, but then Luna remembered this." She points around the now newly decorated and furnished area.

"The men moved all the rubble and debris out and helped install the windows and other things that the cleaning and construction bots couldn't do. It took us several days to get this all done because we were only working on it when that second sun of yours was out. Of course, SAGE did her magic with the furniture and the major designs. Miya, I hope you like it. We made everything neutral colored so that you could put your own personal touches on the place."

Miya doesn't say a word. I can see she is overwhelmed. She walks ahead of me and towards the windows lining the far wall. When she approaches, the window retreats, and I watch as she steps out onto a small balcony. I look around at what they did to the extensive area overwhelmed by the beauty and the meaning behind all of this. I feel tears gather behind my eyes the moment I realize I have a home now. A place to call my own, with Miya by my side. "I don't know what to say."

Tordan bumps me. "How about thanks, you big grumpy ass!"

"I'm overwhelmed and so thankful that you all would do this for me...for us."

Miya runs back across the room, hugging each one of them, talking so fast I can barely make out the words. Kira takes her hand and I watch as they walk around the room together. One took my life and the other one gave it back.

I make my way over towards one of the large couches and try my best not to plop down on it as my legs are trying to give out on me. As I take a deep breath, Miya jumps on me, straddling my waist with her legs. I grab her hips, smiling, enjoying the feeling of her happiness. "Behave, little beauty, or we will break the couch."

DaR yells out, "I think that's our cue, females. Everyone say your goodbyes and let's get the goodies you all bought at the market back on the shuttle. I'm ready to head home and sit on my own couch."

"Hugo, before I lose your attention altogether because of that temptation sitting on your lap, SCOUT left some machines in the outer building for you to look at. When we were packing all the crap out of here, we found crates of cybernetic arms. I think you will be impressed with how SCOUT implemented them onto a hoverboard picker. If they work properly, the results would be astounding, and they fix our personnel problem with getting in the beans. But take your time and get healed. Enjoy a long Lunar rotation with your mate."

I hear them all talking and laughing as they walk out of the room, but my sole focus is on the beauty sitting on my lap, looking at me.

"What's going through that mind of yours, little beauty?"

"Would you have let me go? Do you mean more to me than I do you?"

"I want to say that, yes, I would have let you go. But, honestly, I'm not sure. I believe the moment you would have gotten on that shuttle. I would not have been far behind. The very thought of not hearing your voice or being able to simply see you whenever I wanted tears me apart. I don't particularly like being dependent or vulnerable when it comes to another. You are practically carrying my heart in the palm of your hand. I pray to the Lord of Light that I become a male worthy of you and your love."

"You are pushing yourself too hard. You have nothing to prove to me. I could care less about all these material things. Now don't get me wrong I don't want to go hungry either. But knowing you are always going to be here to catch me if I fall is all I need. I never was one of those girls who dreamed of a prince charming of her own, but in a sense, that's what you are, but in a grumpy version. Are you upset that they did all of this without talking to you first?"

"Are you? I know most females like to make their own marks upon their dwellings."

"Not at all. I think it's fabulous. I never could have dreamed up a space like this. It has all the basics, but I can't wait to put our mark on it, as you said."

"If you're happy, then so am I. I had lived with so little for so long that this seems unbelievable. I'm scared to move out of this spot, worried that I'm dreaming and that you and all of this will be gone."

"I have an idea. I mean, if you're dreaming, we might as well make it a good one."

Miya wiggles her eyebrows at me suggestively and suddenly my cock is rock hard under her. I can feel the heat of her core through the clothes that she has on teasing me. I grasp her hips, rolling them as I rub my cock against her pleasure button. My hands move across her body and under her top, caressing her skin gently. Smiling to myself when I feel her body tremble slightly under my touch. I pull her close, kissing her softly at first, my tongue dueling with hers. She has quickly become my new obsession, as I roll my tongue in a deep caress.

I yank her top off only to see another piece of fabric hiding her breasts from me. Before she can protest, I take a claw and snap it in the middle, my eyes devouring the sight of her sitting upon me. Her full breasts and dark, hardened nipples are only inches away from my face. My long tongue reaches out, flicking one nipple while my hand caresses the other one.

She moans as she squirms on my lap. I lower her down beside me onto the couch, laying partially over her. My hands eagerly look for the clasp that is holding her pants on. Once I discover it, I slide her pants off her legs, dragging her shoes off as I go. Another piece of material hides her hidden treasures from me, but instead of immediately cutting through them, I run my hands up her long smooth legs.

My hands caressing as my lips kiss her soft thighs. She moans when I suck on her swollen pleasure button through this piece of fabric. Her hands reach for my head and I swear it feels like for a moment that she had grabbed onto my horns. The base of where they were is suddenly sore and extremely sensitive.

I slide back up her body, slowly kissing her navel and all around her stomach while I rub the palm of my hand over the soaked material hiding her treasure from me. I take one of my claws, making sure that I don't cut her, and then toss the material to the ground. I retract my claw and immediately sink my fingers inside of her.

Her body lifts up as I rub her button as I move two fingers in and out of her. I lower myself onto the floor and pull her legs over the side of the couch and up over my shoulders, opening her legs completely. Her glistening lips beckon for me to taste them.

I put my hand on her stomach, holding her down as she squirms as I lick her from top to bottom. She makes sounds that spur me on and I go at her like a starved male. Pressing three fingers into her tight folds, my tongue teases her nub as her climax builds higher and higher. I can feel her inner walls start to flutter around my fingers. I bite down gently on her pleasure button while flicking it and she arches up off the couch, screaming out my name.

Nipping the inside of her thigh, I give her a second to catch her breath. My cock is pressed against the shorts so hard it's painful. I reach down, releasing it, and line myself up with her now dripping folds, rubbing myself up and down as she grips my arms, trying to take her legs to pull me closer.

"Don't tease me, Hugo. I need you."

I line myself up and push in slowly. She is wet, but I'm a big male. I rock back and forth, each movement seating me farther inside of her. She is so tight that it's almost painful. This is the most mind-blowing thing I have ever experienced.

Every thrust I make she cries out. I reach between us, flicking her pleasure button again, and I feel her inner walls tighten even more around me. Miya's cries of pleasure pull me along with her as my own release sneaks up on me. I grab her hips so tight I'm worried there will be bruises later. Drained, I collapse, my head laying on her chest as her legs lay limply at my sides.

I have no idea how long we lay here when I hear Miya gasp. I raise my head up only to see her looking at the palms of her hands. Concerned, I pull out of her, immediately missing the feel of her wrapped around me.

The markings on her palms shocked me as I pull her hands towards me. "Where did these come from?"

She points to my head and I reach up, only to find a set of short horns. It takes me a second to get to my feet, but once I do, I pull Miya up with me and then head into the refresher.

I can't believe what I was seeing in the mirror. My horns, I have my horns back. They are not as large as they once were. However, I'm stunned that they have regrown at all…and they are mate marked. The same marks that now match Miya's palms.

I tug her in front of me, my cock still hard, pushing at her lower back as I open her palms up so that I can see their marks in the mirror. Miya looks at me and then up at my horns.

"The marks match. What does that mean? And when did you get the new accessories?" She points to the new horns on my head.

It takes me a moment to rationalize it in my head before I can answer her. "You're my true mate. I had forgotten… My parents were true mates too. She wore my father's markings all over her body. I was always told we could not mate or procreate with another species, but here is the proof that we can."

"What does this mean?"

"I don't know all the answers to that, but I know it links our lifespans. Before long, well, the more we mate, the stronger our bond will be. In time, I will be able to find you anywhere." I pick her up, spinning her around. "Touch them again."

Her laughter fills the room as she grabs onto them again. When I raise her up, she wraps her legs around my waist. I kiss her softly before asking, "I think we might need to strengthen our bond. Do you have any objections?"

"Find the bedroom in this place. Let's see how creative we can get with these marks."

EPILOGUE

T wo Lunar rotations later

Miya

"Hugo!" I yell out. Then talking to myself, "Lord, I have looked everywhere for that man. Where is he?"

"AMI, have you seen Hugo anywhere? I swear these last two days you would think he was hiding from me."

"I have been sworn to secrecy, Miya, however, all will be revealed soon."

I was just getting ready to head outside when I finally see Hugo packing a large container into my old room. He still has moments of weakness, but you would never know it right now, as his muscles flex with the weight of the box he is carrying. I wait until he is through the door before I sneak into the room behind him. Only to stop dead in my tracks. There are tables all around the room, most of them lined with crates. "Hugo, honey, what are you doing?"

He turns towards me quickly. His snarl is quickly replaced by a huge smile. "It was supposed to be a surprise, but honestly, I thought you would catch me before now. This is all for you." He points around the room.

"What is it?"

"According to Alana, it's everything and anything you could possibly need to make your smell good stuff."

He turns away and starts pulling a few things out of the crates, setting them up on the tables. My eyes tear up when it hits me about what he has done. "Hugo stop."

"What's wrong, don't you like it?"

"I love it. I LOVE YOU! How did you do all of this?"

"You have friends in high places and they are already putting their order's in, but say it again."

"I love you."

"I never tire of hearing you say that. I had no idea what that meant before you, and I feel like that four-letter word is not large enough to hold all the feelings I have for you, but until I can figure out a better one. I love you, my little beauty, and I will until the end of all existence. Now come here and let's try out a couple of these tables."

233

THE END

OTHER BOOKS FROM THIS AUTHOR:

The Water Skippers series

Water Skippers

(Kyle and Eden)

A Dragonfly's Whisper

(Nora and Roman)

Earth Shadow

(Lorene and Garret) part one

Shadow Reborn

(Garret and Lorene)

Petal

(Randy and Petal)

Miranda and the Dragonfly King

(Miranda and Tagon)

Stand-alone novel

The Playboy and the Waitress

The Forsaken series
Forsaken
(Lucas and Emma)
Betrayed
(Tavish and Eve)
Forgotten
(Tyberius and Victoria)
Spin off to the House of DaR series

Darverius
DaR
(DaR and Kira)
XuL
(XuL and Brittany)
SoL
(SoL and Alana)
RaZ
(RaZ and Katherine)
A House of DaR Celebration (novella)
Tordan
(Tordan and Luna)
Hugo
(Hugo and Miya)
AvX
(AvX and Ivy)

JENNIFER JULIE MILLER
WATER SKIPPERS SERIES
THE FORGOTTEN SERIES
WATER SKIPPERS
DRAGONFLY WHISPER
EARTH SHADOW
SHADOW REBORN
PETAL
Miranda Dragonfly King
FORSAKEN
FORGOTTEN
BETRAYED
HOUSE OF DAR SERIES
THE PLAYBOY
SOL
RA
CELEBRATION
Gorlan
HUGO

I hope… I have made you laugh, and possibly… even squeezed a few tears out of ya. Writing has been a lifelong dream for me, and our dreams are the only thing we have to build on!!!

So GO for it!!!!

I'm an avid reader myself. I believe there are Dragons, Unicorns, and multicolored Kitty Cats, because our imaginations are our own uniqueness.

I want to thank my family and friends for all your support.

To my readers, thank you for encouraging me to continue writing even though my worlds are a little different.

After all, I'm Appalachian, and I talk Appalachian. Therefore, I write Appalachian. All my books have country girls in them, and that's mainly because I only know how to speak country girl correctly.

Then to the Lord above, whose blessing gave a poor little girl from Ironton a chance to dream!

If you enjoyed this story, or any of my other ones, I ask that you take a few minutes of your time, and leave a review on Amazon, or Goodreads. It really helps new and older authors alike.

If you would like to stay in touch, hear about new releases, give some advice, or just drop a line.

You can find me on Facebook.

Https://facebook.com/JenniferJulieMiller.

On Twitter.

Https://www.twitter.com/jenniferrick

Or email me at:

Jenniferjuliemiller@gmail.com

Follow me on bookbub. **Https://www.bookbub.com/profile/jennifer-julie-miller**

Follow me on Amazon.

Https://amazon.com/author/jjm5325903

And sign up for my email if you want to learn more about Darverius and DaR's twenty-two plus sons.

Http://eepurl.com/cfrL8X

DAR

Kira

In the blink of an eye, my whole world has collapsed around me. Headed towards my dream vacation, I was snatched right out of the air. My husband, the love of my life, was destroyed right in front of my eyes. He fought bravely, trying to protect me from a horror neither one of us could have ever imagined. I find myself standing in the spotlight on a stage. Mutilated and tortured, the blood from my body flowing freely down my legs along with my will to live. Piercing yellow eyes emerge from the darkness, but even the shadows can't hide his imposing form. Gentle, but terrifying arms reach out for me and within their embrace, can I find the will to live again?

DaR

I am a bad ass, known throughout the galaxy for my brutality as a ruthless and feared commander. With that being said, somehow, I still got coerced into purchasing a slave. My eyes fall upon a small female whose very essence and eternal light is leaking out of her onto the floor below her. I watch in awe as she accepts her fate, willing her nightmare to be over. I almost turn away from her and the unnecessary cruelly in this room, but the very thought of her dying on that floor surrounded by the very monsters that have done this to her disgust me. I walk up among the beings surrounding her and pull her from the stage, daring, or should I say, hoping, they try to do something about it. The moment I put her in my arms, everything changed. The attachments I have avoided my whole life become unavoidable. Will this damaged slave be able to replace the shadows in my life? One thing for sure is that I will destroy the entire universe to keep her safe. No one touches what's MINE!

XUL

Brittany

All my dreams and wants were stolen from me in the blink of an eye. Awakening, in the middle of a nightmare, I realize I'm being sold like an animal to be studied and dissected in the name of science. Then tragedy strikes, leaving me abandoned and sick. I am only moments from taking my last breath when strong arms pull me from the darkness. I thought it was a blessing that he had found me, the green man who had haunted my dreams. I let myself believe, for just one moment, I might find a small piece of happiness in this unknown world. But what is the old saying? *'Don't count your chickens until they hatch!'*

A blood sucking parasite is eating me alive, literally, and no matter what, I'm not going to survive this horror story. My body is failing me. I beg him to let me go; I just want the pain to stop, but he won't listen. He holds me down and I struggle weakly against his immense strength, choking as blood fills my lungs. When I can't fight any more, Death opens its arms and invites me in.

XuL

My harsh, brutal features have deterred all females, no matter the species. I long for companionship and love. Then I find her, my Kismet, the only one made just for me. The one precious thing I would worship above all others. But the fates are cruel, especially to a male like me.

I am being forced to destroy the fragile bond that has formed between us, as I have to make the hardest decision of my life. One that will make me lose her either way. I hold her small, struggling body against me. Tears flow down my face as she begs me to stop. My heart is crushed as I watch the light leave her beautiful eyes. Upon her final breath, I vow not even Death will keep what's mine.

SOL

Alana

The question is, do I allow this dark moment in time to rob me of the life I could possibly have here? I have never known such horror or fear. If I hadn't experienced it myself, I would have never believed any other living thing could possibly do this to another. The scars may be gone on the outside now, but they will remain forever in my soul. They tell me I can never go back, all that I have ever known is gone. Where does this leave me in the world of monsters? He beckons me, promising me…the fairy-tale… the impossible dream. Everything I have ever wanted to hear! But I don't know if I'm strong enough to go forward as long as the shadows of our past pull me backwards.

SoL

I knew she was withholding the truth from me. I had no idea who I held in my arms until it was almost too late. The moment her true essence was revealed to me, my body reacted, reaching out for the one thing I had been searching for my whole life... my Inamorata. The very mistress of my heart and now that I have finally found her. I will follow her through the sands of time... no matter how long it takes. I will find my way back to her... because she is MINE!

RAZ

Katherine

How do you go on when all of your wants and dreams have been destroyed? My loved ones were snatched right out of my hands, leaving me alone in a world of unknowns and terror. I'm lost in the in-between with no familiar paths to follow until the sound of a heartbeat and a whisper draws me back to the land of the living.

RaZ

The moment I laid eyes upon her face, I knew there would be no distance I wouldn't travel to make her my own. Unknown forces try to steal her from my very arms and even if I have to fight the very essence of her world, the universe, or the very Gods we pray to. Nothing will stop me from making her MINE!

FORSAKEN

Lucas and Emma

Katherine's parents

The one question she often asks herself is *why*. Why has she never been enough? Why doesn't anyone truly want her? She was reminded daily that she was nothing but a worthless girl and only another mouth to feed. The last time she saw her family was the night they dumped her in a ditch on the side of the road and left her to die.

A kind woman took her out of that ditch and gave her a home. Her new family was every girl's dream until a single poisoned scratch took it all away. Emma was tossed away again, becoming a prisoner and a slave to her circumstances. The one person the Cook enjoyed beating regularly. The day Cook sold her body, all of her hopes and dreams were destroyed. But one fateful night, after fighting for her life, she escapes this, Hell.

He finds her on the brink of death, naked, beaten, and barely alive. She thinks he is the Angel of Death, someone who will save her, but he is a real monster. Did she just trade one Hell for another? Will the memories he steals from her dreams soften his heart enough to make him care for something more than himself? Or will he turn her away, just to *Forsake* her, like all the rest?

BETRAYED

Tavish and Eve

It seems the ones we love the most are the first to Betray us! One such Betrayal cost me everything: my home, my dreams, and almost my life. The second I started running, I knew I would never be who I was or may have wanted to be. All of my choices were taken away with two last breaths, hers and then my own.

The dreams of my youth were destroyed because of the selfishness of others. I fear my life will become nothing but a cold existence of shadows and detachment.

The poison consuming my very soul is nothing but an excuse for me to lash out at the unfairness of it all. It's exactly the justification I need to deliver the pain others have inflicted on me my entire life. Will the emotions of my untried youth destroy my future as I'm forced into a world I truly don't understand?

My own mind has become my worst enemy, and my fragile heart can't withstand another break. I know he's a deceiver, a devil in disguise, sent to collect my grieving soul. He is the real monster my mother warned me about under the bed. If I let him, he will destroy me in the end with his mischievous smile and lying angel eyes.

To be loved is the only dream I have left, but we all know Betrayal is the one thing you can always count on to crush you.

FORGOTTEN

Tyberius and Victoria

(DaR's father)

I have known this evil was coming for me my whole life, but that doesn't mean I have looked forward to it! I have run from every sign of the darkness, even to the point of being invisible to the ones around me. I've spent my whole life lurking in the shadows of my family. Keeping myself separate from the ones I love, living my dreams, and wants through their eyes.

I had become so wrapped up in their worlds trying to ensure their happiness that the day he appeared in front of me. I never once questioned what I was supposed to do. The one thing my family could always count on is that I'm loyal to fault. Even though I made sure never to get too attached because I was terrified the darkness would take them also, it will do anything it can to defeat me. My goal is to survive and to finally see the light.

I have prayed to every God, for this to pass me by, only to know they can't answer. This is my destiny. I will suffer agony unlike anything my mind can imagine, but to be worthy of the light. I need to find a way to face this darkness.

I will never show him an ounce of weakness, but I scream silently for help. I refuse to let him win because he wants me here for eternity. A soul withered in ice, and loneliness, Forgotten in this room of horrors.

All the stars line up for us one time or another. I just have to wait my turn.

TORDAN

Luna

They stole my dreams, my hopes, my very identity, and I had no idea. Years went by and I did everything I was told, I was always the perfect specimen, and the perfect lab rat. I was dissected, even maimed all in the name of science. Then one day a strange smoky voice entered my head, and I knew things were not as they seemed. He promises me that he will never leave me, but my new memories tell me differently.

Tordan

What is it about that one person that attracts you like no other? My mind can't figure out that riddle, but the moment I laid eyes upon her I knew my life would never be the same. When I finally held her in my arms, I swore I would never be without her again.

If they think they will get me to comply by using her to control me, they're right. What they don't know is…I will tear this compound, and all that's in it apart, to protect what's MINE.

THE PLAYBOY AND THE WAITRESS

Jenna

I was always told never to forget that I was worth something, too!
We all know that every little girl dreams of her knight in shining
armor. A man who will ride up and save her from the evil things
trying to destroy her. Then, of course, we all know they live
happily ever after. My knight was untouchable... A Playboy, a
man who stole my heart right out of my chest and with very little
effort on his part. Unfortunately, he was also a man whose world
I would never fit in. You can take the girl out of the country. You
can dress her in nice clothes, have her smile beautifully as you
parade her on your arm, but you never really take the country
out of the girl. I reach out for the brightest of stars... only for
him to leave my heart in pieces, crumbling at my feet.

Dage

I watched her for weeks. Every smile she bestowed on me captured me in a way no others had. Circumstances throw us together over and over and no matter how many times I hold her in my arms, it's never enough. I didn't know what I was missing until she walked away. I know, I can't have them and her... so who will lose?